Bondi's Brother

A Story of Love, Loss, Betrayal and Liberation

by
Irving Roth
and
Edward Roth

BONDI'S BROTHER

Published by:

SHOAH EDUCATIONAL ENTERPRISE

14 Gordon Drive

Williston Park, NY 11596

Tel: (516) 741-8920

E-mail: irving.roth1@verizon.net

Cover Design........................Susan Sussman, Abby Graphics LLC

Copyright 2004 by Irving Roth and Edward Roth

ISBN-10: 0-9787649-0-0
ISBN-13: 978-0-9787649-0-6

First and second printing 2004
Third printing 2005
Fourth printing 2006
Fifth printing 2007
Sixth printing 2008
Seventh printing 2009
Eighth printing 2009
Ninth printing 2010
Tenth printing 2011
Printed in the United States of America

This book is dedicated to the memory of my brother Bondi and the one-and-a-half million children who perished with him in the Holocaust

"From out of ashes...
Faith
Vision
Rebirth!"

Rabbi Abner L. Bergman

About This Book

Bondi's brother is so much more than a survivor - he is an eloquent narrator and a powerful witness. The artistry of terse prose, etched images, and richly woven threads of character and story bring this distinctive Shoah memoir into vivid, compelling focus.

The atrocities are sketched subtly, but without flinching. Nobility and courage appear too infrequently, but are never absent - least of all from the narrator. Irving Roth reminds us that survival in Auschwitz demanded luck, strength, ingenuity, the kindness of some and the indifference of others, and providence. He teaches us that with courage, realism, love and hope, one can move on in life. But this is something one never gets over.

The way he and his son have told it, the story and the lessons, will endure as well.

The Rev. Peter A. Pettit, Ph.D.
Director, Institute for
Jewish-Christian Understanding
Professor of Religion
Muhlenberg College
Allentown, PA

Who's Who in the Story

Anu and Bondi

Ervin Roth

Grandpa
Shimon

Grandma
Rachel

Uncle Harry

Apu and Anu

Itzu

Andras and Gabi

Bondi

Edit, Aunt Klara and Zoli

Table of Contents

Introduction

Succos – Festival of Booths -1981. Sunlight drifted in through the bamboo poles overhead, illuminating his face. The dark rings under his eyes disappeared. Pine needles gave the air a sweet smell. The remains of a fruit platter sat between us. We were alone - the perfect time to hear the story. I had heard little pieces, but the stories were always detached, as if it happened to somebody else.

"Dad, close your eyes. Now think, you're back in Europe. Tell me everything…from the beginning."

His eyes squinted and he held his head. His forehead creased.

"You know, I was the first person in the family to be born in a hospital."

Slowly, he told me what happened.

When we got to the part where the Hungarian Police gathered the Jews of Zdana, I asked, "Did you try to hide or escape?"

"Sure we tried." He paused for a few seconds. "But Bondi wouldn't go with me. So I went with Gabi and Uncle Moritz."

"Enough! That's it." A hand waved in my face. He shook his head. He jumped up from the table and walked out.

Twenty-one years later my father walked into my house holding a loose-leaf filled with notes.

"I want you to write my story. I want the grandchildren to know what happened. Will you do it?"

"Will I do it? Of course I'll do it!"

The painful process began. I'm taking notes, picturing the German army marching under Dad's bedroom window; he stops and goes into the den.

I ask my mother, "What happened? Is Dad coming back?

1

"No, I think he's done."

Often, my dad would mention someone's name or remember a conversation, get choked up and leave the room. If I pushed too hard he'd say, "I can't. What do you want from me? It's too much."

It was tough to watch my father go through the intense and often agonizing process needed to write this book. But he persevered. I hope I didn't let him down. I wrote this story because of my dad's strength and resolve to record his memories. It is his personal history of the Holocaust. The dialogue between characters is based on his recollections. Sometimes he remembered phrases; other times entire conversations. I have tried, as much as possible, to capture the essence of my dad's experience along with the nuances of his language. It was challenging since his native tongues are Slovak, Hungarian, Yiddish, Hebrew and German. It was also hard to resist a natural desire to revise the past based on my relationships with family members I know or knew. Many appear very different from the way I knew them. "Remember" I'd say to myself. "This is about Dad, not you." I have tried to remain true to my father's words.

Although this story is mostly about loss, it is also a story about survival. My dad survived. He came to America, married, served in the U.S. Army, attended high school, college, graduate school, and raised a family. My brother and I were raised a little differently from our friends. We inherited some of our father's fears of uniforms, marching bands, smokestacks, sirens, and barbed wire. We were constantly reminded that the whole world could fall apart in a moment. But my dad was never bitter or filled with hatred. Ironically, my dad emerged from Auschwitz an irrepressible optimist. It's our responsibility to make sure this doesn't happen again. And Dad has never stopped believing that mankind is up to the task.

Edward Roth   *October 2003*

Chapter 1

Erzi

I was born in a hospital in Kosice, Czechoslovakia. The country doesn't exist any more. A lot of the places I'm going to tell you about don't exist anymore. In 1929, Kosice was a fine place to be born. Nobody in the family was ever born in a hospital. But when my brother Bondi was born, my mother wouldn't stop bleeding. And if not for Grandpa Shimon racing to get a doctor, my mother would've died. So with me, they decided I should be born in a hospital. Grandpa Shimon said I was born into luxury.

Erzi was my mother. She was Hungarian and Catholic. She had light brown hair and brown eyes. She wasn't fat, but big boned and very strong. Erzi wore dresses with lots of buttons, especially on Sunday when she went to church. Anu, my real mother, hired Erzi to bring me up. It's a good thing too, because Anu accidentally spilled hot tea on my arm when I was six months old. I would have been scalded even worse if Erzi hadn't quickly grabbed me and put me into an ice bath.

I was always moving, so Erzi didn't have it easy. Tree branches kept ripping my shirts. My shoes were magnets for mud. Erzi was tough. If there was dirt on the floor, she would come looking for me. And if she caught me, I'd get a *potch* (smack). But Erzi had soft spots, too. If I got banged up or was bleeding, she never yelled. She didn't like to see me hurt. Tears also worked with Erzi, but I didn't overdo it. She could tell when I was faking.

Erzi knew everything about being Jewish. She knew not to mix dairy and meat and how to bake *challah bread* and what you were allowed to do on the Sabbath and what things you weren't. She made sure I said the *Shema* (prayer affirming the unity of God) before I went to sleep. She even knew some Yiddish.

Still, Erzi was a religious Christian. She went to church every Sunday and sat up against the big glass windows. I waved at her whenever I passed by the Church, and when she could she'd wave back. She celebrated all the Christian holidays. At Christmas time there was a tree decorated with tinsel and candles in her bedroom. I rode my tricycle round the tree and put presents under it for Erzi and her daughter, Olga, who usually lived with Erzi's parents. Erzi wasn't married. I couldn't figure out how she could have a child.

Anu once said to Erzi, "You shouldn't be sleeping with the mill workers. It isn't proper…and you could get pregnant."

Erzi turned red. "That's easy for you," she said. "You've got a husband that sleeps next to you every night."

Anu dropped the subject, but it stayed in my mind a long time.

I was born in Kosice, but we lived in Udavske. Udavske was a small village. There was only one main road and it wasn't paved. At the end of the road was a metal bridge that went across the Laborec River. The metal slats of the bridge pounded like a drum whenever a rider made his way into town. Most of the time the bridge was silent, except on market day when it thundered with the horses' hoof beats.

Peasants came in horse-drawn wagons packed with chickens, geese, and fish swimming in small tubs. They brought baskets of carrots, string beans, apples, and pears. The whole town was filled with food. They traveled down the main street at dawn and by the end of the day sold everything. They went back the same way they came, stopping first at the tavern owned by Mr. Tobias. It was a dark wooden place with hewn benches and tables and a whiskey counter. The peasants loved to drink. Even though he did good business from the peasants on market day, it was only one day a week. Mr. Tobias barely made a living.

The peasants smelled like the earth. They were sweaty and strong and carried knives. The knives were long and sharp. They used their knives for everything. After work they'd sit down wherever they were. They'd cut wild mushrooms right off the tree trunks (the forests were filled with mushrooms), slice pieces of salami and wedges of cheese. The salami smelled better than the incense used in the Holy Temple. I would stare at the peasants and wished I could join them. Erzi had to drag me away. She would whisper in my ear, "I don't care what they're eating. They're a bunch of no good drunks." Erzi stayed clear of the peasants. And so did I.

Erzi saved me many times. Once during the summer it rained for a week and the Laborec River overflowed. By Sunday the rains stopped and it was hot. The Jewish kids of Udavske hurried down the main road barefoot in swimming shorts making lots of noise. They cut in near the tavern next to the church with the big windows and cooled their feet in the muddy ground. They ran between my father's office and Mr. Meleznik's apartment. Mr. Meleznik was my father's good friend. They turned into the covered veranda that connected all the company apartments and screamed, "Bondi, Ervin," as loud as they could. My brother and I slipped out of our house ready for action joining the band of hooligans. I was five years old and barely kept up with them. We ran through the gardens behind the apartments. We were screaming so loud, with such high pitched voices that the priest stopped his sermon and looked outside. The grass was wet and slick under our feet. The river was normally wide and not very deep. At night from my window I listened to the sound the current made as the water traveled gently through our village. The riverbanks were covered with large smooth colored pebbles. In a few spots gray sharp railroad gravel mixed with the pebbles.

Because of the storm, the river had doubled in width. The water poured over the embankments and reached as far as the orchards. As I got closer to the river I heard the water rushing downstream. It was dark and muddy. It sounded like somebody breathing fast with short breaths. The older boys threw themselves into the water. They were screaming and splashing. I couldn't tell that the river was not just wider but also much deeper. My feet touched the water, and I slid down a hill. The water was freezing. I thrashed my arms, but I was sinking and everything was black and upside down. I'm not sure how long I was under, but out of nowhere, a powerful hand gripped my wrist. An arm wrapped around my waist. In an instant I was snatched from the water coughing and crying, pulled tight against a woman's bosom. I clung desperately to Erzi's Sunday dress bouncing up and down as she carried me home.

Erzi stayed with us until 1939, when I was ten years old. That's when Jews were no longer allowed to have Christians work for them.

When I was in Auschwitz, I kept thinking about Erzi. I imagined that she would come to the camp and say that there was a big mistake, that I was her son, that I didn't belong there, and she would take me out of the camp and hide me in her house. I would play with her daughter and decorate her Christmas tree, and she would hold me against her bosom because she loved me like a mother.

After the war when I was seventeen, I saw her again and she cried and hugged me for a long time. She opened a soft leather wallet that Anu had given her as a present. Inside was a worn picture of my brother Bondi and me. That was the last time I saw Erzi.

Sometimes I dream about Erzi holding me with her strong arms against her bosom, crying.

Chapter 2

The Tailor's Son

Anybody who was anybody got new clothing for *Passover*. When I was five and a half I became somebody. Anu brought me to the city for new shoes and a suit.

Humenne was the closest city to Udavske. It had paved streets and lots of stores. Even though *Passover* was early that year, the snow had almost all melted and the roads were clear. Still, it took over an hour in a carriage pulled by two horses to get to Humenne.

Anu held my hand. I pulled her arm hard and tried to break away, but she didn't let go. We were on a mission. It was to the shoemaker and the tailor.

The shoemaker measured my feet. It was no big deal. All I had to do was take off one shoe and place my foot down on a wooden measuring board. The shoemaker wrote down some notes on a tiny pad he kept in his shirt pocket. Anu selected fine brown leather to be made into shoe-boots. He gave me a balloon and we were done.

The tailor was not the shoemaker. His name was Sobel *bacsi* and he was a difficult man. He put me on a wooden platform and insisted I stand perfectly still. I swayed once to keep from falling and it was too much for him. He was annoyed that my mother was busy picking out fabric on the other side of the store and left him to deal with me alone. I was annoyed because I wasn't used to having anyone poke me. I resisted and we struggled. Finally, Anu heard the tailor's cursing and came over. She promised me a treat if I behaved and I did. I knew a good deal.

The tailor measured and pinned the fabric that was draped over my head like a shroud. Then he re-measured and re-pinned and made marks with chalk and soap and ordered me to stand up straight, relax my shoulders, drop my arms, and turn around and around. He pricked me with pins and stuck me with a pen. When he was done torturing me, he pointed with his crooked finger and said, "Go!" No balloon, no candy, nothing. Just 'Go!' I jumped off the platform and landed so hard the floor shook.

The tailor's face turned red. I ran out of the store with Anu after me. I pitied the kid who was unlucky enough to be his son.

Before my sixth birthday the lumber mill in Udavske closed. Grandpa Shimon and Apu, (my father) decided to go into business together. My grandfather knew everything about forests and lumber. Apu was a smart businessman and accountant. There was nothing keeping us in Udavske. Humenne was closer to forests and mills and it had a big Jewish community.

I started religious school in Humenne. We studied the old fashioned way: *kometz aleph aw, kometz bais baw* (ABC). Everything I learned, I learned by heart. My teacher *Reb* Gross, was in his fifties. He was tall and thin with a gray beard. He never smiled. People said it was because his daughter died when she was giving birth. He was soft-spoken and didn't use a paddle, keys, or a belt for discipline. Still, he kept a long stick made out of birch on his desk and if he needed to, he knew how to use it.

A stocky boy with bushy sidecurls tucked behind his ears sat right behind me. His name was Chaim Sobel, the tailor's son. One afternoon, I had to go to the bathroom, which was behind the schoolhouse. When I got back and sat down, Chaim pulled my chair out from under me. Everybody laughed. It wasn't funny. It hurt, but I let it go.

Then, small paper airplanes landed on my desk. Next spitballs were shot at the back of my neck, all from the hands of Chaim Sobel. He made the class laugh again by pointing out that my curly hair made me look as if I had a lamb on top of my head. I sat in my chair and I said nothing. The *Mishna* says, "Be slow to anger and quick to forgive," so I controlled myself.

At the end of the day I was walking home with my friends. Chaim wasn't done. He sneaked behind me and kicked my books out of my hands. My books went flying. That was it. I had enough. I turned around. Chaim the tough jokester was laughing, that is, until I punched him in the stomach. He doubled over. Then I picked him up and threw him to the ground. He hit the ground hard, and it sounded as if his head hit a rock. Chaim wasn't moving. I yelled his name and when he didn't answer, I ran off.

I didn't tell my parents what happened and I didn't hear anything about Chaim over *Shabbos* (Sabbath), so I figured he must be okay. If there was a problem I would have heard. But when Chaim didn't show up for school the next day, I got worried. And it was for a good reason. I found out that Chaim was at home, sick with a head infection.

Chaim told his father it was my fault. And I told my father the truth. Apu was strict, but fair.

Apu said to me, " I know he got what was coming to him. But did you have to hit him so hard?"

I said, "I didn't hit him so hard. He fell. He must have hit a rock or something."

Apu said, "It doesn't matter, they're going to blame you."

I said, "That's not--- ."

"Fair?" Apu cut me off. "Who told you everything's fair?"

"*Reb* Gross."

"*Reb* Gross?" Apu's eyes widened.

"Yeah. *Reb* Gross. He said Abraham told God he couldn't kill everybody in Sodom and Gomorrah because it wasn't fair."

Apu's lips thinned. "That's because Abraham was talking to God. God is fair. Not human beings. Human beings are a totally different story. You think it was fair that Joseph should have been put into jail because of Potiphar's wife? Or that Jewish babies should have been thrown into the Nile? Does that sound fair?" Apu's eyes were burning. He lifted his voice. "Ervin, does that sound fair to you?" I was going to say something back, but I could tell Apu didn't want me to answer. Apu looked away from me and was silent. It was his sign that we were done speaking.

The next day Sobel *bacsi*, the tailor, showed up at my house. He came to talk to Apu. They sat in Apu's study for half an hour. I was scared. I hid under the dining room table and waited for the tailor to leave. From under the table I saw two pairs of legs walk towards the front door. One pair of legs left the house.

I came out from under the table and walked over to my father with my head down.

Apu said, "You're lucky. Thank God the tailor's son is getting better."

"What did he want from you?" I asked sheepishly.

"He wanted money to pay for his son's doctor's bills." Apu walked away from me and went back into his study.

I stood at the door to the study and asked, "What did you do?"

Apu said, "I gave him what he wanted." Apu shut the door.

When Chaim Sobel came back to school, he didn't sit behind me. He sat on the other side of the classroom. He wasn't a jokester any more, and I could tell he was afraid of me. Still, I wasn't proud about what happened. Even though I didn't feel I did anything wrong, I felt guilty. And worse, *Passover* was coming and I would have to get a new suit from Sobel *basci*. Seeing Chaim's father was going to be painful.

Anu brought me into the shop. Sobel *bacsi* was busy taking measurements. He looked up to see who entered and his face tightened. I tried not to let our eyes cross. In the back of the shop a boy was leaning over a worktable. Slowly, I made my way over to the boy. It was Chaim sweating over a suit jacket. He didn't look like a jokester. He looked like a kid who knew to listen to his father and was working hard.

"Hey Chaim, what are you doing?" I asked.

Chaim looked up and saw it was me. I thought his heart stopped.

"Making…ah… buttonholes," he answered.

"Could you show me how to make them?" I asked.

"I guess. If...do you really want to learn? " he said.

"Sure, I've always wanted to know how to do them." A smile came to Chaim's lips.

Many times in Auschwitz, when a button fell off my gray and blue striped prisoner's jacket or when it ripped I was able to fix it. And I did it the way Chaim Sobel showed me.

Chapter 3

Grandpa Shimon

Problems. There were always problems. But Grandpa Shimon always came up with a solution. Everybody came to Grandpa for help. He was very smart. I loved watching Grandpa's face when he was thinking. I could tell when Grandpa had an idea. I'd see his gray mustache move to one side and his large forehead crease. Then his eyebrows pinched together and his eyes grew big. His lips puckered like they were going to whistle. Then he'd shake his head and smile.

We had a problem around *Passover*. The *Passover* wheat was stored in the attic for six months. Eventually, the wheat would be made into flour and then into matzah. Mice had gnawed through the burlap sacks and made their homes in the brown kernels. Grandpa Shimon had to keep the wheat free from vermin. What we needed was a foolproof trap.

First, he went up to the attic and stared at the wooden walls and floor planks. He pushed boxes of *Passover* dishes and small crates around and measured everywhere. Then he made a drawing; the kind an engineer would make. It was very precise with lengths, widths, and thickness neatly labeled. Even after the drawing was finished, Grandpa didn't rush to make the trap. He said, "You measure twice and you cut once." He took me to the woodpile in the back of the house for the selection. Grandpa ran his fingers along each piece of wood. He checked for moisture, knots, and wormwood. The wood had to be straight and even. If a piece of wood was too moist he threw it into a pile on the left. If it was diseased or eaten by termites, he threw it into a pile for firewood on the right. He smelled each piece. He said, "Wood should smell like the forest." After the wood passed his inspection, he gave it to me for final selection. We took turns cutting the wood to the proper sizes. Each cut piece was carefully checked against the drawing. The scraps and wood-chips were added to the pile on the right for firewood.

The trap was very clever. Wheat and cheese were placed at the rear of the trap in a little box. The mice would enter through the front and would choose a path to get to the food. Along the path the weight of the mouse would cause a door to slam shut and a brick to fall. There were ten separate paths to the bait. The trap could catch many mice before it had to be emptied. Every few days Grandpa and I would check the attic. We dumped the dead animals into the dung heap near the barn. The trap worked and the *Passover* wheat was kept pure and clean.

Grandpa Shimon solved other problems. He had a friend named Moshe Gittleman. He was a milkman who also sold prune preserves and other delicacies. They played pinochle together. Mr. Gittleman was always having money problems and Grandpa was always loaning him money. Every time Grandpa gave him money, Grandpa wrote a legal note for the amount of the loan, but he left the due date blank.

My father said to Grandpa, "Why do you waste your time writing all those notes with Gittleman? You know he's never going to pay you back. Just give him the money as charity."

Grandpa said, "I can't. He's the *gabai* (synagogue official). And we play cards together every Tuesday. If I give him the money, it would change our relationship. A loan he understands."

Mr. Gittleman never had the opportunity to repay the loans. Both he and my grandfather were murdered in Auschwitz.

In 1939, the *'Nuremberg Laws'* (Nazi anti-Jewish Laws) came to Czechoslovakia. Jews had to wear yellow stars. They couldn't wear fur coats or anything with gold. They couldn't sit on a park bench. The laws also made it illegal for a Jew to own a business. Our family lumber business was very successful. We made railroad ties and shipped them all over Europe. Grandpa Shimon came up with the idea to have Mr. Meleznik take over our lumber business. Albert Meleznik was a good friend of the family. He lived next door to us in Udavske and worked with Apu and Grandpa for the National Lumber Company. I played with his kids. He was the witness at my parents' marriage, and his signature was on their marriage certificate. He had a kind, familiar face and always gave me candy when he visited.

Mr. Meleznik was invited to our house. Anu put plates of strudel, nut torte and sponge cake on the dining room table. Grandpa gave Mr. Meleznik a cigar to smoke and sat him down at the head of the table.

Anu went into the kitchen and left the men alone to drink, smoke, and discuss business. I stood in the hallway and watched.

Grandpa said, "Albert, you know the problems that we Jews are having now."

Mr. Meleznik washed down some cake with coffee and said, "Yes. It's awful the way the world is."

"If things go on the way they're going, being Jewish and running a business will be very difficult," Apu said.

"You see Albert, we want to know if you can do us a small favor?" Grandpa continued. Mr. Meleznik's eyes opened wide.

His cheeks were red. He puffed on his cigar. "Sure Shimon, we're old friends."

"It's not a big deal, really just a technicality. We'd like to put your name down as the official owner of our company. You wouldn't have to do anything, just sign a few papers," Apu said.

"And of course you'd be paid for this," Grandpa added.

Mr. Meleznik had a big smile and reached over to Grandpa. He put his plump hand on Grandpa's shoulder. "Shimon, whatever you want me to do, I'll do. Like I said, we're friends." Grandpa poured slivovitz into three glasses and the men shook hands.

Mr. Meleznik signed the papers and the business was transferred to his name. New stationery was printed. Every month Mr. Meleznik received a large check from the business. Grandpa and Apu were grateful. Our life continued the way it had, just one more bill to pay.

Three months later Mr. Meleznik was back in our house. He sat at our dining room table drinking coffee and eating cake. He needed to discuss the business arrangement. He said it wasn't right that he was being paid a monthly salary, especially since he was now a partner. As a partner, how could he be paid like a worker? No, he should get half of the profits every two weeks. Apu and Grandpa couldn't do anything. Albert Meleznik was the legal owner of the business. Every other week he collected half the profits.

Four months later, Mr. Meleznik came to our house again. He said he was very happy with the way my father and grandfather managed *his* lumber business. They were good and loyal employees and even though it was a Christian company, there was no reason to fire hard working Jews. They would receive a fair salary for their work and be paid in a timely manner. Mr. Meleznik was an old friend of the family. On his way out of the house, he saw me standing in the hallway. He reached into his pocket and gave me some candy. Grandpa and Apu were sitting at the dining room table. Their faces were white, their eyes opened wide and their hands were shaking. But I wasn't worried. I knew that Grandpa would figure out a solution.

Five years later, in 1944, Grandpa saved me and a whole group of Jews from freezing to death. We were brought to a brick factory in Kosice, Hungary. We stayed in drying sheds in the yard outside the factory. The sheds were huts without walls where the clay bricks were stacked for drying. It was cold. At night the wind picked up and I thought we were going to die. We huddled together trying to stay warm. I watched Grandpa walk around the brickyard. He was counting to himself. His mustache was twitching and his eyes grew big. He picked up a rusty metal pipe and scratched a few lines on the ground. There were bricks thrown all over the yard. He told the men in the yard to bring him as many bricks as they could. An hour later, Grandpa had built two walls that met in the shape of a 'V'. We huddled inside the protected area. Our own body heat made it warm enough to sleep and we survived the night.

Two weeks later, we were packed into cattle cars. We were told we were being resettled. Through the cracks in the car's floor I stared at the tracks below. We traveled hundreds of miles. I thought about all the railroad ties needed to hold the rails together. I thought about Mr. Meleznik selling our lumber to the Nazis. But I didn't mention it to Grandpa.

The train stopped and the door slid open. We were rushed into lines and told to leave our belongings on the side of the tracks. We moved up slowly in rows of five. A Nazi guard asked Grandpa what he did for a living. Grandpa figured that if he said he was a pensioner, he would get a better job in the concentration camp. They wouldn't make an old man dig ditches or drain swamps. Grandpa said he was a pensioner and was told to go to the right. I was told to go to the left. I asked the *kapo* (inmate camp enforcer) where they took my Grandfather. He said, "Up the Chimneys."

Chapter 4

Anu

Uncle Itzu trusted Anu. He was her favorite brother, the last of eight children. I always remembered him having stomach problems. One morning he came to breakfast holding his belly.

"Ilonka, I'm sick," he said.

"You look terrible. You're sweating. I'll get Father and he'll call for a doctor." Anu got up to leave.

Itzu grabbed Anu's arm tightly. "I've got a doctor. He's taking my appendix out... today!" Itzu moaned.

"What? Are you---" Anu raised her voice.

"Shh," Itzu covered her mouth. I've arranged everything. A friend of mine is a surgeon here in Humenne and..." Itzu moaned again.

"You're crazy. A local doctor? I'm calling Father. He'll get you a real surgeon."

"Ilonka, No! I'm going to the hospital. I've taken care of it. And if you tell anyone..."

Anu held Itzu in her arms like a child. She cried. He placed his finger against her lips.

Itzu was always treated differently from the rest of the family. He was the youngest child and the whole family spoiled him. Grandpa allowed him to go to the university in Prague and Itzu got a Doctorate in Engineering. He had lots of friends, Jews and non-Jews. Today, you'd say he was connected. He was independent and did his own thing. When he was home, he respected his father and went along with most of the Jewish customs and rituals, but when he was out of the house, he felt free to do as he pleased. Anu always covered for him.

The local doctor did the surgery. When the operation was finished, a messenger was sent to the house. He said that Itzu Rosenwasser was recovering from surgery. If we wanted we could visit him. Shocked by the news, everyone ran to the hospital. The hospital wasn't old, but still smelled like alcohol and disease. There were rooms with beds filled with sick people pinned under their sheets. Even though it was light and warm inside, I hated the place. To me it smelled and looked like death. Itzu was unconscious, lying motionless in bed. Anu placed her hand on Itzu's forehead. She ran to a nurse. "My brother has fever!" she yelled.

The nurse said, "Please, please, relax. Patients very often have a little fever after surgery. Your brother will be fine."

"I would feel better if someone looked at him."

The nurse took Itzu's temperature. It was high. The nurse felt Itzu's abdomen and noted that it was hard. Anu asked what it meant. The nurse didn't answer. She walked away quickly. A minute later, two doctors arrived. They asked the family to wait outside while they examined the patient.

The operation had not gone well. We learned that Itzu's friend, the surgeon, was drunk during the operation. Itzu was bleeding into his abdomen. The doctors did not want to do anything. They felt reopening the wound was too risky and hoped that the bleeding would stop by itself. We stayed by Itzu's bed watching for improvement. In the morning Itzu was still unconscious. His face was the color of ash and his belly was swollen. Grandpa sent word to a surgeon from Presov to come as soon as possible. It was no use. By the time the surgeon got the message, Itzu was dead.

Saturday night the body was brought to our house. Members of the Burial Society arrived to do the purification of the body. Apu, my brother, and I had to leave the house since we were *kohanim* (priests as defined in the Torah) and couldn't stay under the same roof as a corpse. Sunday morning was a beautiful sunny day. A buddy of Itzu's said to me, "What a waste. On a day like today Itzu and I would have gone on a hike."

Itzu's friends carried his casket on their shoulders over a mile to the end of town. They carried the casket up a steep hill. Itzu was buried in the Jewish Cemetery. He was twenty-five years old.

At first, Anu refused to believe that Itzu was dead. She kept calling his name as if someone was going to answer. She set a place for him at the dinner table. When he didn't show up, she announced, "Itzu must be sick. He has a bad stomach you know." Low wooden stools were brought to the house and the mirrors were covered with sheets. Candles were lit and neighbors came by to comfort the bereaved. It was only then that Anu seemed to understand that Itzu had died. During the seven days of mourning she didn't speak. She barely moved. She wouldn't eat anything and if she was forced to eat, she vomited. After the mourning period, Anu hid in her bedroom. For weeks she lay in bed, too weak to get up. Grandpa and Apu called doctors to the house. Anu got worse. Specialists came to examine her to see what could be done. They gave her medications, herbs, and vitamins. Nothing helped. Anu was wasting away, and I was scared. Erzi was already gone because gentiles weren't allowed to work for Jews anymore. Uncle Itzu had died, and now my mother was going to die. My father and brother were busy reciting Psalms. They told me to do the same. It would help Anu.

The Psalms worked; months went by. Anu still spent most of the day in bed, but her condition stabilized. The conditions for Jews in Humenne, however, got worse. Without Erzi, the laundry piled up and meals were skipped. Grandpa and Apu couldn't run the house. Anu had no choice. At first it was as if she was sleepwalking. She boiled some eggs in a pot. She washed the dishes. Sometimes a dish would slip from her hands and crash on the floor. I was in charge of cleaning it up. Anu started to prepare simple meals and do the laundry. Slowly she began to talk. Once or twice she held my hand. There were moments when I felt as if I had my mother back. But they were only moments. Most of the time, Anu just did what was needed to function and nothing more. And I never saw her smile again.

Chapter 5

Bondi

It's very difficult for me to speak about my brother, Bondi.

A benefit of staying with Cousin Zoli in Zdana during the summer was that my Godfather lived close by. His name was Gutman *bacsi*. He didn't have any children, so he didn't feel bad about spoiling me. Just before I returned to Humenne, I stopped at Gutman *bacsi's* house. He said he had something special to show me. He opened up a closet and pulled out a shiny black case. Carefully, he placed the case into my hands and said, "Nu, open it. It's a present." He was very excited. I unlatched the lock and pried the case open. Inside was a violin.

On the train ride home, I kept the violin on my lap cradled in my arms. It was too fragile to place in the storage bin above the wooden seats. I stared at the case and dreamed about being a violinist in an orchestra. I opened the case many times and rubbed the smooth lacquered dark wood with my fingertips. I examined the black chin rest and tightened and loosened the horsehair bow. I softly picked at the strings. Music. Okay, it didn't sound like much, but it was the first time I touched a real violin.

When I got home, I couldn't wait to show my mother what Gutman *bacsi* had given me. I pulled out the instrument, jammed it under my chin, grabbed the bow and made believe I was a violinist. The next day Anu brought a gypsy to our house. The gypsy had long black hair tied together in a ponytail. He had a mustache and dark complexion. His shirt was colorful and his pants were black.

The gypsy snapped his fingers and said to me, "Okay, okay, let's get going. Pick it up. Let me see."

I was nervous. I pushed the violin under my chin and tightened my fist around the bow ready for my first lesson.

The gypsy waved his hands in front of me. "No, no, no. There's no hope. I cannot teach him." He turned towards Anu and said, "Shame, a

20

beautiful violin."

The gypsy looked around the room. "There is maybe someone else?"

I was crushed. My mother hesitated and looked away from me. "He has an older brother."

"Bring him here to me. Let's see if someone in this house will play violin."

Anu called for Bondi. My brother walked into the room holding a book of Psalms. He kissed the book and placed it on the fancy end table.

"What do you want Anu?" he said, staring at the gypsy.

"I want you pick up the violin," the gypsy answered.

Bondi looked towards Anu for direction and then at me. Anu nodded and he reached for the violin my Godfather had given me. My brother pulled the violin from my hands and placed the black chin rest gently under his chin. He held the bow between his delicate fingers and swept the hairs over the strings. Clean notes came out. "Yes! This one is good. This one I will teach." The gypsy was delighted.

The gypsy came to our house once a week for two years. Bondi learned fast and practiced for hours. He loved music and loved to show off how well he played. He played everything; classical pieces, haunting gypsy melodies, and Klezmer wedding songs. I couldn't believe how fast his fingers moved and couldn't understand how he knew where to place his fingers on the black wooden neck. One time the gypsy and my brother played together. I sat on the couch in the living room with a soccer ball on my lap and watched them; their chins bobbed up and down, their arms moved back and forth and their mouths looked like they were going to cry. When they finished playing, the gypsy was out of breath. He said to Bondi, "Everyone, everyone is crying. Even angels in heaven."

Just before Bondi's *Bar Mitzvah,* Anu's cousin died. A *Torah Scroll* was brought from the synagogue to be read at the house of mourning. Apu was a *baal koreh* (Torah reader) and read the Torah. When my father was asked again to read *Shabbos* afternoon, he said his throat hurt. Apu

21

asked Bondi to take his place. My brother had a beautiful voice and read the Torah without making a single mistake. Everyone in the room ran up to him after he finished and told him how well he read and how Apu should be proud to have a son like him. My father, who rarely showed emotion, placed his hand on Bondi's shoulder and kissed him on the forehead.

After his *Bar Mitzvah*, Bondi got even more religious. Of course he put on *teffilin* (phylacteries) every morning and prayed. But he also chanted Psalms every day and completed the whole book every *Shabbos*. When he started to learn *Talmud*, he fell in love with learning. He began every conversation with, "It says in the Talmud…" When he studied, he looked just like a *rebbe* (rabbi), with his thumb going up and down as he read through *Rashi* and *Tosafos* (famous commentators on the Torah and Talmud). Everything he did had some religious reason or significance. I didn't share his love for Torah. Bondi would beg me to learn, or at least try to get me to recite Psalms, but there was no way. I preferred to play soccer and hang around with my friends. Sometimes Bondi would get angry at my lack of interest and try to force me to learn. But it was no use. If he hit me, I hit him back harder. He learned quickly not to use force.

Even in Auschwitz Bondi kept on praying. While marching out with the horses in the early morning, Bondi had his eyes closed with his lips trembling through the morning prayers. There were plenty of religious boys in our group, but Bondi was the only one who prayed every day. Sometimes Bondi was so wrapped up in prayer he didn't pay attention to the *kapos* or the guards and got a beating. I tried to get him to concentrate on what was going on in front of him, but it was no use. I fasted on *Yom Kippur* (Day of Atonement) and recited the prayer of *silent devotion* on *Rosh Hashanah* (Jewish New Year), but otherwise I was focussed on staying alive. Bondi was focussed on serving God. He was watching out for us in the world to come. I was in charge of making sure nothing happened to us in this world.

On our Sunday march back from the fields into the camp, Bondi would temporarily stop praying. As we walked through the main gate of the camp, underneath the words '*Arbeit Macht Frei*' (Work Makes You Free), we heard music. Forty to fifty musicians in gray and blue striped prison uniforms sat to our right. It was a sight. Famous Jewish musicians from all over Europe were practicing and performing classical pieces. During the week we got back to the camp after dark, so we didn't get to hear the music. But on Sunday, we worked until noon. As we made our way back to the barracks we marched to Brahms, Beethoven, Mozart, and of course Wagner. We marched five abreast, and I made sure my brother was always next to me. Bondi wanted to stop and watch the violinists play, but I pulled him along with the group. Maybe I should have let him stay and watch. He had more in common with the musicians than the rest of us working with horses and dredging swamps. But if he left the formation, the *kapo* would have beaten him. As we continued past the orchestra, Bondi's head bobbed in time with the music and his fingers pressed and twitched on an imaginary violin in his hand. His mouth twisted, and he looked as if he was going to cry. His face was contorted, but at least his eyes were open and he wasn't praying.

Towards the end of the war I got separated from my brother. I ended up in Buchenwald where a Czech *blockaelteste* (inmate senior barracks supervisor) was in charge of my group. He had a friend who was a violinist and somehow managed to steal a violin for him to play. We were starving. Still, this man came one night and played an original piece of music that he composed in his head in a cattle car on his way to the concentration camp. The tempo echoed the beat of the train wheels clanging against the breaks in the tracks. When he finished most of the boys clapped. I thought of my brother. How he would have enjoyed the music. How happy Bondi would have been to touch a violin again. The melodies he would have played. Most of the boys clapped, but I was crying.

Chapter 6

The Police

The *Wehrmacht* (German Army) was everywhere. It was the day before my tenth birthday, September 1st 1939. They poured into Humenne on their way to Poland. Day after day they came. Trucks filled with soldiers, artillery cannons, panzer tanks, motorcycles, even soldiers on bicycles. The procession continued day and night. I spent hours watching the movement from my bedroom window. It was a spectacle. The truck lights and the rumble of the tanks had a hypnotic effect and I was drawn outside to get a closer look. I found a good spot to be a spectator, not far from my house, on Hlinka Street. A soldier was walking out of Gelb's grocery store eating an apple. I followed every movement he made. He was wearing a gray uniform with a thick black leather belt around his waist and high shiny black boots. From his belt hung a gun in a holster. He was young and tall, clean-cut in his uniform. His skin was smooth and his cheeks were red. He had a nice smile. I was about to go over and ask him his name when a Jew with a white beard caught the soldier's eye.

"Hey old Jew, what are you doing on the sidewalk?" he barked. I was so surprised by the way he spoke I held my breath.

The man stopped and didn't look directly at the soldier. "I'm walking," he said quietly.

"Jew, I can't hear you. Your beard is getting in your way. Come closer so I can hear you."

When the man moved closer, without warning the soldier kicked him in the leg with his boot. The man fell to the ground. The soldier asked, "Now what did you say you were doing, Jew?"

The man buried his face in his hands.

The soldier continued to smile as he stepped over the man and crossed the street. I wanted to go after the soldier and kick him. These people were guests in my town. Where was the policeman to arrest this criminal? I was shaking. I ran to the man and helped him up. The soldier joined two other soldiers and disappeared into a stream of uniforms.

The man got to his feet, brushed off his black coat and rubbed his leg. He thanked me for helping him and asked me my name. He told me to watch out for the soldiers. As he limped away, I heard him curse the Germans. At the far end of Hlinka Street I saw a few policemen helping soldiers push a stalled truck. I went back to my bedroom to watch the troops. I pulled the window shade down and peeked through a crack. I couldn't risk being seen. The soldiers looked different. They were disfigured. Their boots were blacker. Their faces were sharper. Their eyes were indifferent.

That night, I heard German being spoken near our house. Some soldiers were flirting with our neighbor's daughter. I wondered if they knew she was Jewish. I had trouble falling asleep because of the noise. Every German word reminded me of that soldier. I couldn't get his smile out of my mind. I watched the clock tick. Finally, I fell asleep.

When I was in Auschwitz, a guard thought I wasn't working hard enough. I hadn't had a regular meal in so long it was a miracle I was able to stand. The guard came over to me and kicked me in the shin with his boot. As I fell to the ground I got a look at his face. He was smiling. I thought about his face again when I was lying on my shelf in the barracks, but only for an instant. Even though it was noisy and I was squeezed next to my brother, I didn't have trouble falling asleep.

Chapter 7

Sonia

Sonia and I had a lot in common. She lived on my block in a house her parents rented from a Jewish family. Her father was university educated like my father. We were the same age and were in the same class. We walked to school together and usually I carried her books home. Sonia wasn't good in math, so I helped her with homework and studied with her before examinations. Sometimes we studied at her house, sometimes at mine. She had black hair and a dark complexion. Her cheeks were always pink and she was beautiful. I liked Sonia very much. My life couldn't have been any better.

Everything changed in 1939. Slovakia was now an independent country with a Catholic priest named Joseph Tiso as its president. In school, every classroom had a crucifix hung on the wall, and we recited Christian prayers before our morning lessons. Each morning I prayed that England would attack Germany and make Czechoslovakia a country again, a country that liked Jews. My father was worried about me. He told me to be careful in school and when I was walking around Humenne. Anti-Semites were riling up the people. He heard that Jewish children were getting beaten up. He also didn't think it was a good idea that I was spending so much time with Sonia. He figured her parents wouldn't be happy their daughter was being seen with a Jewish boy. I told him that I would watch out, that I could handle myself pretty well if I had to, and if Sonia had a problem she would tell me.

On the first day of school in 1940, my brother was in a rush to get to class, so I didn't get to walk with Sonia. Still I was excited; I knew that I would see her in school. Bondi and I walked together until he turned off towards the path to the high school. As I got closer to the elementary school, I saw some of my friends standing outside the entrance gate. A school official was inspecting every student. Most, he let through the gate and some were turned away. When I got to the gate, the official said I couldn't go in. I asked him why and he said, "Jewish students were not permitted to enter the building." I was taught to be patriotic, proud of my country, and proud of my school. And now I wasn't welcome in the building. I joined my friends off to the side of the gate and waited. About a minute later I saw Sonia walking towards the gate.

As she passed through the gate she saw me and asked, "What are you doing?"

"They won't let us in…" I said. She continued into the school courtyard. "…because…" I yelled, but Sonia didn't turn around. She disappeared into the building.

Eventually, I went home. Bondi was already sitting at the dining room table reading. He wasn't upset or anxious. He was happy that he wasn't going to school. Now he would have more time to study Talmud. I didn't share his feelings. Sonia was sitting in school, and I was sitting at my dining room table watching my brother read. In the afternoon I headed out to play soccer. Maybe I would feel better if I was running around. And maybe I would see Sonia coming home from school. On my way to the field I met up with a few of my Jewish friends. We walked past the elementary school, but I didn't see Sonia. When we got to the soccer field, there were some kids kicking a ball around. We asked them if they wanted to play. They told us to go away. We didn't belong there. Jews didn't belong there. We weren't going to force them to play with us, so we left the field and went to a vacant lot behind the synagogue. The teams were smaller, but I got to play soccer.

Two days later the Jewish parents got together and set up a school in the building where I went to religious school. Finding teachers wasn't a problem since many of the teachers in the public school were Jewish and now out of work. Within a week, the school was in session and I was studying and doing homework. Sonia lived only four houses away from me. The physical distance between us was very small, but our worlds divided. We almost never saw each other and even when we did, we didn't speak.

After the war, I went back to Humenne. A few of my Jewish friends had also survived the concentration camps. We formed a club called *Hashomer Hatzair* (a Zionist youth organization) and did everything together. One day we went to the dairy to pick up milk and I saw Sonia walking towards us carrying a 2-liter milk can. I wanted to run over and carry it for her. But I couldn't. What could I say to her? While I was in

Auschwitz, she was in school. She did homework. She ate dinner. At night she went to sleep in her bed. Sonia was even prettier now than she was before the war. But I walked past her and filled my milk can. She would never understand.

Chapter 8

Deportation 1942

It was Friday night. The men walked to the synagogue to pray. It was crowded and hot, and *services* took a long time. The men looked worried. On the way back, the streets were dark and still. At home, my father chanted *kiddush* (prayer over wine sanctifying the Sabbath) and then blessed Bondi and me. After we washed our hands, Apu said *hamotzi,* (prayer before eating bread) and handed out pieces of *challah bread.* I helped Anu bring noodle soup to the table. She was weak and shaky, but she made a good meal. After removing the soup bowls, I brought out the roast chicken, egg barley, and carrots. Grandpa and Apu stared at each other. Their eyes expressed worry and fear. We ate in silence.

The town crier had been giving us bad news for months. Corner to corner, he beat his drum announcing the 'New Laws.' He told us what was coming, but we didn't know when. It could happen at any time. That night there was no dessert. We rinsed our hands at the end of the meal and recited *grace* quickly. Apu checked the lock on the front door and we went to bed.

They came about midnight. There was a sharp knock at our door. "Open up," they commanded. We stood in the hallway frozen in our nightclothes. The door shook and they pounded again. Grandpa told us to get away from the door and stay in the dining room. I watched for the *Malach Hamaves* (Angel of Death). "One minute, one minute," Grandpa yelled as he opened the door. A neighbor of ours named Andil stood in the opening. He was wearing the uniform of the Hlinka Guard. Andil was always quiet and reserved, and I was surprised to learn he hated Jews. Behind him was a policeman with a gun in his hand. Apu was standing next to Grandpa. He was holding our exemption card, which indicated that we were still needed as essential workers. Apu pushed it in front of Andil's face. Andil looked at the card suspiciously. Our names were listed in a column on the left side of the card.

"Who do you have in the house?" Andil asked.

"There's me, Joseph Roth," Apu said pointing at a name on the card. "Then there's Simon Rosenwasser and Rachel Rosenwasser, Ilonka Roth, Ondrej Roth, and Ervin Roth. Six of us you see, all on the card."

"There's no one else in the house?"

"No. No one. Just the people on the list."

"Okay, they can stay. They have exemptions…for now," Andil said turning to the policeman.

The men left and Grandpa shut the door. He locked it and checked it a few times to make sure the door was securely locked. Grandpa and Apu joined us in the dining room. They were out of breath and flushed. Even though it was warm in the house I was chilled, so I pulled my robe tight around my body. We heard noises outside. It was the sound of marching. In the middle of the night Humenne was alive. I ran to my bedroom window and saw wagons and horses, people with suitcases walking, mothers holding babies, Jews dressed in *Shabbos* clothes, police, and Hlinka Guards. I saw my Aunt Malvene and Uncle Moritz who lived in the neighboring village pass our house without looking up at our window. This was the great exodus that the town crier had announced. They were going to be resettled somewhere. They were going to work camps. We knew we were the lucky ones.

I said *Shema* under my blanket that night, not to muffle the noise outside, but for security. In the morning I got up early and crept into the living room. Grandpa, Apu and Bondi were already dressed and praying. We weren't going to synagogue. We weren't going to step outside. The streets were quiet. Around 10 o'clock there was a knock at our door. Apu opened the door a crack and peeked at the visitor. It was Rozi Klein, a Jewish woman from Hungary who was visiting her relatives in Humenne. Apu rushed her inside. She was a petite woman who walked with firm steps. My family crowded around.

"It's terrible. They've put everyone into the synagogue. They're locked inside, and the police won't let them out even to use the toilets," she said.

"How many people were taken?" Apu asked.

"I'm not exactly sure, but it looks like thousands. The synagogue is packed. There's no room to move, and the air is hard to breathe."

"Is there anything we can do?" Grandpa asked.

"That's why I've come. I'm bringing water, tea, and coffee in buckets to the synagogue. Do you have any tea or coffee?"

"Yes. We have both. Ilonka, let's heat some water in the large soup pots," Grandpa said.

Cooking is not permitted on *Shabbos*, but this was no ordinary *Shabbos*. Rozi Klein carried heavy buckets filled with coffee and tea to the synagogue. She walked about the town, unafraid because she had a Hungarian passport so the deportation laws didn't apply to her. We hid in our house.

Mothers, fathers, elderly grandparents, little children, infants, our neighbors - suitcase in hand, entered the synagogue where they remained for almost two days. Hungry, frightened, degraded, and disoriented, they waited in the stagnant air. Finally, cattle cars arrived in the station. The Jews were herded into the cars and speeded off. The Jews of Humenne disappeared.

Sunday night we opened our doors and went outside. The town looked the same. The monument dedicated to General Stephan still stood in the Town Square. The City Hall and Social Security building remained clean and stately. Trains were on schedule coming in and out of town. Jewish stores taken over by non-Jewish neighbors continued to do business. Their signs and awnings remained. All that had changed was that instead of 2,000 Jews, there were now only 200. They were the families of those Jews considered vital to the city's economy. What that meant was that the non-Jews still needed some Jews to run the large businesses.

A group of us gathered outside the synagogue. When we opened the doors we found a *churban* (defilement). My eyes stung from the smell of urine. Diapers were left on the floor under the pews. Remnants of clothing: a sock, a shirt, a belt, left in haste, forgotten on the staircase. My synagogue was defiled with human excrement. The High Holidays were coming. Some non-Jewish workers were hired and together we swept and scrubbed the synagogue to make it ready for the holidays. On *Succos,* Jews sing *Hallel* (Psalms of praise). Did it make sense to praise God? The Book of Life and Death was opened and I was being judged. It was only a matter of time before we, too, would be deported.

Chapter 9

The Auction - Summer 1942

It was a dark and cloudy morning. Rain was imminent. A crowd gathered in the cold outside the Rabbi's house. I stood behind a bush near the street unnoticed. Two men dragged out furniture. I heard a man yelling, "Do I hear ten, do I hear ten?" in a singsong voice. People in the crowd yelled out numbers. It looked like a carnival. The furniture was pushed to one side. The man held up tablecloths and pillows and pillowcases and bed spreads. One by one they were put in a corner of the yard. Finally, they bid for the house itself. It didn't go for much. The bidders moved forward, anxious to claim their goods. Then they walked away. Most of the crowd went on to the next house. Left in a heap in front of the Rabbi's house were the Rabbi's books. They were holy books and they were piled like mountains everywhere - books that sat on our Rabbi's bookshelves, that he studied from and *paskened*, (made legal decisions). Books I would have kissed if they fell from my hands. They were shoveled into a huge pile on the front lawn. Some books fell from the workers' hands and they kicked them towards the main pile. I watched them pour kerosene on the books and light the pile on fire. Smoke, thick and black, filled the air. Orange flames danced and licked the covers. I saw the covers light up and for a moment the titles were illuminated. My eyes burned from the smoke and tears dripped down my cheeks.

There was a large Talmud on the top of the pile. It had a brown leather cover decorated with a gold design at the borders. The fire was spreading quickly. The books were in flames. In another second the Talmud would catch fire. I had to do something. I jumped out from behind the bushes and grabbed the large volume pulling it close against my chest. A worker spotted me and yelled. "Hey, what are you doing? Get away from the fire." I turned around and ran. First I ran down Church Street, past the synagogue, then to Hlinka Street, onto my block and finally home. Chilled from sweat and out of breath, I made it back to my house without being followed. I placed the giant book on the dining room table. It was tractate *Sanhedrin*, the tractate that deals with legal proceedings of the Supreme Court in ancient Jerusalem. The book was still warm from the fire and I warmed my hands on the cover. Even though it smelled from kerosene and was smudged with soot, I hugged the book in my arms. It felt good to hold one of our rabbi's books. I kept thinking how proud I'll be to give Rabbi Ehrenreich his Talmud when he returns from the work camp. I saved a part of his library and I would guard the book until the rabbi came home.

Of course, this was not to be. The huge book did not accompany me on the cattle car to Auschwitz. And Rabbi Ehrenreich never came home from the camps.

Chapter 10

Bribery

We were lucky to still be in Humenne after the deportations. But it was only a matter of time, and we knew it. After all, there were quotas to be met, and eventually no amount of money or connections would be able to save us.

It was a Monday morning and I recited the morning prayers with Grandpa Shimon in the *Beis Hamedrash* (House of Study). We had just a *minyan* (quorum of ten men) since there weren't many Jews left in town. As we were leaving, two policemen were standing outside.

"Excuse me, do you have your Exemption Card?" one of the policemen asked Grandpa.

"Sure, I have my card," Grandpa answered showing the men the yellow paper. They didn't look at the card.

"I'm sorry. It's not valid. You'll have to come with us," one of the policeman said in a curt but cordial tone.

"Not valid? That's impossible. Of course it's valid. Don't you see what it says here?" Grandpa was annoyed and tried to show the policeman the card again. The policeman gently pushed Grandpa's hand aside.

"Please, calm down and come with us," one of the men said.

"Where are you taking me?" Grandpa asked so that I could hear.

"To jail. But just for a short time. Don't worry, you'll be fine."

Holding Grandpa's arms they walked away. As they walked I heard Grandpa repeating to the men, "You know this is all a mistake. I have a valid card."

I ran home to tell my father what happened, but the family already knew. Grandma had just been picked up by the police and escorted to jail. Apu called the Chief of Police, who could be bribed, but he said it wasn't a local affair; it was out of his hands. The orders came from Bratislava and there was nothing he could do. So Apu and I went to see Mrs. Sanger. Apu went into her house and I waited outside.

Mrs. Sanger was about thirty years old and married to a man who owned a taxicab. She lived in the same house as her in-laws not too far from us. With blond hair and a striking figure, she looked like a Slovak version of a pinup girl. We heard she had a special relationship with Alexander Mach, the Minister of the Interior, and helped save others from deportation. She was our only hope of saving my grandparents. Inside the house she shared with her in-laws, Mrs. Sanger called Bratislava to find out if anything could be done for my grandparents. Phone calls went back and forth. Everyone in the family was given a job. I was running back and forth to the jail to make sure that Grandpa and Grandma didn't disappear. For a time the phone lines went dead and we thought time had run out. But by the end of the day, thanks to Mrs. Sanger's efforts, my grandparents were released from jail. Apu rewarded Mrs. Sanger for her help. She and her family survived the war.

We were now desperate. We knew we had to leave Slovakia. But no country would let Jews in, so there wasn't anywhere to go. Still, Apu and Grandpa came up with a plan. Apu was born in Zdana, which was now part of Hungary. That made Apu Hungarian, entitled to Hungarian citizenship. His Hungarian citizenship would extend to my mother, Bondi, and me. With the proper papers we could be repatriated and cross the border into Hungary. The problem was that Hungarian citizenship would not extend to my grandparents, so Apu decided they would just have to cross the border illegally. To complete the plan, Anu and I traveled to Budapest to make arrangements to smuggle my grandparents into Hungary. On the train, as we crossed the Hungarian border, Anu cut the yellow stars off our jackets since Jews of Hungary were not required to wear a yellow star.

When we got to Budapest, Anu and I went to her uncle's house. It was a four-story building with a restaurant on the ground floor. Uncle Mordcha Stern was the owner of one of the best kosher restaurants in Budapest. Anyone who was in Budapest during those years would have heard of Stern *Bacsi's* Restaurant. Horty, the Regent of Hungary, had a son who ate at the restaurant on *Shabbos* just for the mouthwatering

36

cholent, (stew). The restaurant made Uncle Mordcha rich and he was well known as one of the main supporters of the *Belzer Rebbe.* Unfortunately, Mordcha and his wife Ilonka had no children of their own, but their large house was always filled with guests. Anu's sister, Aunt Friedush and her family were living in one apartment when we got there and we moved in with them. Zoli, Aunt Klara's son, was sent to study at a Jewish high school in Budapest and was also living in their apartment. Zoli and I shared a bed. Aunt Ilonka, Uncle Mordcha's wife, heard of a young girl left behind in Budapest whose parents had been deported. When she saw the six-year-old child, she fell in love with her and wanted to bring her home. But Judka wouldn't go without her sister and two brothers. So Uncle Mordcha and his wife adopted all of them. Judka and her three siblings lived in another apartment in Uncle Mordcha's house. Judka got whatever she wanted. One day she wanted to go ice-skating. Since I was the only one in the family who knew how to skate, I had to take her to the local rink and make sure she didn't hurt herself. It was fun having a little sister.

Friday nights and *Shabbos* afternoons the restaurant was filled with *orchim* (guests). Uncle Mordcha would hold a *tish* (banquet) and feed an army of poor people delicious kosher food. While we were staying with Uncle Mordcha, word came that the *Belzer Rebbe* was coming to Budapest. Uncle Mordcha helped pay for an elaborate plan to have his *Rebbe* smuggled out of Poland and brought to Palestine. The plan worked. The *Belzer chasidim* were not going to let their *Rebbe* die at the hands of the Nazis. The *Rebbe* left his wife and children and his closest *chasidim* behind in Poland. He had his beard shaved and was dressed in an SS officer's uniform. Together with his *shamos* (sexton), *Reb* Shapiro, and a real SS officer, the *Rebbe* made it across Europe to Budapest.

One afternoon, Uncle Mordcha went around and told all of his waiters, workers and relatives to meet him downstairs as fast as they could. A sign marked "closed" was put up outside the restaurant and the front doors were locked. In a few minutes everyone was standing around him and he was so excited he could barely speak. He said, "The *Rebbe's* coming here to Stern *Bacsi's.* He'll be here within the hour so let's get moving. I want everything prepared for him, just so." Like a machine, the restaurant went into motion. The floor was swept and counters wiped. Tables were pushed together and covered with white damask tablecloths. Fancy napkins were placed around the tables and a special cushioned chair was brought into the dining area. The crystal chandeliers were turned on, and everyone was busy with one job or another. We nearly finished when the Rebbe and his *Shamos* came to the door.

The *Rebbe* was a slight man, dressed in a long black coat and black felt hat. His beard was growing back, and the way he looked I couldn't imagine him pretending to be an SS officer. Uncle Mordcha ran to the door and holding the *Rebbe's* arm walked him into the dining area. The *Rebbe* was guided into the large chair at the head of the table and a huge glass bowl of peach preserves was placed in front of him. He was given a silver spoon, and he scooped out a single peach. After he said the blessing the *Rebbe* ate the fruit. He then scooped out another peach and gave it to Uncle Mordcha as *shraim* (sharing food from the plate of a Chasidic Rabbi is considered a good omen). Slowly every person made his way up to the *Rebbe* and got a peach. The *Rebbe* cleared his throat. He said, "God will continue to protect the Jews of Hungary. May God bless you and keep you. May He cause His countenance to shine upon you and be gracious to you. May God lift up His countenance and grant you peace. And let us pray for *Moshiach* (Messiah) to come speedily in our days."

The *Rebbe* stood up and Uncle Mordcha and *Reb* Shapiro escorted him to the small vestibule in the front of the restaurant. A taxi pulled up and the three men left to the railroad station. From there the *Rebbe* traveled to Turkey and finally to Palestine where he survived the war. I got a "blessing" from the famous Belzer *Rebbe* and it came in handy in the camps. I wish my brother and grandparents had been with me in the restaurant. Many times when death was near I would say, "No! You can't touch me. I have a "blessing" from the *Belzer Rebbe."* His "blessing" didn't just help me. It helped everyone in the restaurant that day. Every one of us survived the war. We were lucky, unlike the *Rebbe's* wife and children who were murdered in Treblinka.

Chapter 11

To Zdana

The plan was working. Grandma and Grandpa were being smuggled into Budapest and we were on a train with most of our belongings on our way to Zdana. But, first we had to cross the border from Slovakia into Hungary. We were told that at the border, the Chief of Customs was notoriously dishonest. A suitcase was prepared. Inside was placed: four cured salamis aged in natural casings; paper bags filled with dried apricots, prunes, cherries, almonds, cashews, and filberts; wrapped in towels were two bottles of *slivovitz* (plum brandy), two bottles of vodka, and a bottle of brandy; pushed into the remaining spaces were blocks of chocolate. It weighed a ton and was more valuable than diamonds. It was too risky for Apu to take the suitcase off the train. A man holding a heavy suitcase must have something of value inside. A policeman might stop him and search the bag. And Anu was in no shape to help. Bondi wasn't strong enough to carry the suitcase and was too timid to successfully deliver it to the Chief of Customs; so I was chosen.

When the train stopped, my father went over my instructions.

"Remember, look casual - like you know where you're going. Walk straight into the Customs building. Avoid any policemen. Inside, ask for the chief. Hand him the suitcase and after he opens the bag tell him you need him to wave the boxcar through."

I grabbed the leather suitcase handle and picked up the bag. It was bulky and hard to carry. As I walked down the steps of the car, I turned back towards my family. I wasn't sure I could do it. I started to return to my seat. My father shook his head and motioned desperately with his hands for me to get going. Walking from the car to the building I felt as if the entire world was watching me, that the police were just waiting for me to try to bribe the Chief of Customs - waiting to arrest me. But no one stopped me. I was inside the building and saw a door marked Chief of Customs. Just before I could knock, a policeman appeared and said, "Boy, where are you going with that suitcase?"

"In to see the Chief of Customs," I whispered.

"That's a big mistake," he said with a grin.

"Why?"

"Because if you go in there with that suitcase, you're not going to come out with it."

"I didn't answer him and knocked on the door.

A large, heavyset man with drooping jowls opened the door. "What can I do for you," he asked?

"I'm here to give you something." I placed the suitcase in front of the man's legs.

"What's in there, boy?"

"It's a present for you sir." The man picked up the suitcase and opened it up on his desk.

"Nice. Very nice stuff," he said. "Is there anything I can do for you?" he asked.

I could barely speak from nervousness. "Yes. If you could, I would appreciate it if you could wave our car through the border."

"Sure, let me just put away this bag." The man closed the suitcase and picked up the bag as if it was a feather and placed it under his desk. Together we walked outside to the train. The Chief spoke to the engineer, and I ran back to my car. As I was going up the steps of the train, I heard the policeman yell behind me, "Hey, what did I tell you." I ran to my seat.

Chapter 12

Yellow Star

At last we were all in Zdana. Aunt Klara took us into her home and treated us like the royal Hapsburgs. Aunt Klara was a saint. With dark hair, sturdy torso and dark complexion, she looked like her sister Friedush, only taller and gentler. Klara's in-laws lived with her from the time she married. They were demanding and needed her all the time. No one ever heard her complain. When her son Zoli was living with Friedush in the city of Satoraljaujhel, Friedush was short of money. Because of the war her husband Harry couldn't find work. So, Aunt Klara sent Zoli food. But not just for Zoli; enough for Friedush, Harry, and their daughter Judit. That's how Aunt Klara was - a saint. Besides Zoli, Klara had a 9-year-old daughter named Edit. She had two braids that rested on her shoulders and a cute face that was always smiling. Edit and her mother were inseparable. It was fun being around all the relatives and especially my cousins, Gabi and Zoli. As members of a small soccer club they were eager to have another zealot join their team. The combination of soccer, my cousins and no school made Zdana seem like heaven.

Unfortunately, Apu hated slouches and didn't share my love of soccer. He made arrangements for Bondi and me to leave Zdana to study at a Jewish boarding school in Mishkoltz. Apu also felt he should work and make money. So he and Anu arranged to go to Budapest where he could find a job. On their way to Budapest we were dropped off in Mishkoltz. Bondi and I were miserable from the first day. The classes were in Hungarian and we spoke Slovak. We missed our family. Sleeping in a dormitory with one hundred boys was no consolation either. The food was lousy, and sitting on hard long wooden benches for every meal made the experience even worse. They said the food was kosher, but who knows? The worst day of the week was *Shabbos*. I was used to having a real *Shabbos*. In the boarding school, no one washed their hands before eating bread, and no one sang songs or recited *grace* after meals. The little praying they did was short and without feeling. Most of the kids didn't even dress up in *Shabbos* clothes. It wasn't the *Shabbos* I was used to in Hummene. I complained to Bondi that the school wasn't

Orthodox. He answered, "It was hardly Reform." I wasn't a saint like my brother, but I was still observant.

One Sabbath eve in the middle of January 1944 we received a postcard from Anu. She wrote that Apu came down with typhus and was in the hospital. As soon as he was better they would return to Zdana. Bondi and I read the postcard a few times together and stared at the card in silence. Apu was never sick. Finally, I said to Bondi, "What are we doing here? Apu's sick and the rest of the family is in Zdana. That's where we belong."

"I hate this place more than you do, believe me," Bondi said. "But what are we going to do? This is where we are. And I'm sure there's a reason we're here. It's probably a test. I'm sure it's a test. That's how God works. Everything has a reason."

"Maybe it's a test, but the test isn't that we stay here. God probably wants to see if we can make it back to Zdana by ourselves," I responded.

"I doubt it. Apu brought us here," Bondi said. "And we're staying here."

"If Apu knew what this place was really like, he never would have sent us here in the first place."

"But we *are* here. We'll make the best of it. I'm sure, God willing, Apu will get better and he'll send for us. The war will be over and we'll go back to Humenne. End of discussion."

Sometimes Bondi sounded a lot like Apu and it bothered me. I wanted to believe that everything would work out, but I couldn't.

More postcards came from Budapest and Apu didn't get better. He got sicker, much sicker. One Saturday night in March, the school had a Purim party followed by a dance with girls. Such a dance would have been extraordinary in Humenne. My brother was shocked. I wasn't offended and enjoyed talking to the girls. But when we woke up Sunday morning, Bondi and I had another reason to be miserable. News reports spread that the German army had entered Hungary. We ran from the

Nazis in Slovakia, but they followed us to Hungary. Parents called the school to speak to their children. Special arrangements had to be made because Jews could no longer travel freely. The school quickly disbanded, leaving Bondi and me not knowing what to do. Anu was depressed, Apu was sick, and we were stuck in Mishkoltz. Finally, a telegram came from Zdana. Aunt Klara wrote that she hired a peasant to get us and he was already on his way to Mishkoltz. Within hours the peasant showed up wearing a rough linen shirt and even rougher pants. If anyone asked, we were his children. It seemed a little strange that a peasant would have kids dressed like schoolboys, but at least we all had similar coloring. He carried a sack filled with black bread, bacon and salami. On the train he ripped off pieces of bread and cut slices of meat to share with us. It smelled great and my mouth watered, but we didn't eat a thing. We traveled like real Hungarians, without identification papers. The train took us to Czan and from Czan we walked across the bridge into Zdana. The peasant shook our hands and wished us luck.

At Aunt Klara's we were greeted by bad news. Apu was in a coma. The family was involved in a discussion as to where Apu should be buried. Should he be buried where he was in Budapest or brought to Zdana? Or maybe he could be brought to the family plot in Humenne. I couldn't listen to it. Apu wasn't dead and they already had him buried. A *minyan* was brought together and we changed my father's Hebrew name from *Yosef* to *Yosef Chaim* (the word life was added to his name). I was glad we did something to help my father. We also needed to do something to help ourselves. By now all the Jews in Hungary had to wear a yellow star on their outer coats. Bondi and I had been through this before and we knew what was coming. But the Jews of Zdana were stubborn Hungarians and wanted to believe they were safe. They said Hungary was different from Slovakia. My father would have taken charge and done something, but he was dying in Budapest. Without him, no one could come up with a plan. I spoke to my relatives about what happened in Humenne and pointed to the yellow star on my jacket for emphasis. No one listened.

Chapter 13

Decisions

Passover was coming to Zdana. Grandpa Shimon organized a group of men to bake *matzah* (unleavened bread). We made sure the house was free from *chometz* (leavened bread). *Passover* was a lot of work, but it kept us busy. A postcard came from Budapest. It said that a miracle occurred; Apu was out of a coma and improving. Who knew that changing Apu's name to *Chaim* would work so quickly? I wondered what would happen if every Jew added *Chaim* to his name. We celebrated the good news along with the holiday of freedom. But with the German army in Hungary, the mood remained tense.

The day after *Passover* an order was issued that the Jews from the villages and small towns were to be brought to large city ghettos. I wasn't surprised. My grandparents considered their options. They were old and tired. Being smuggled into Hungary wore them out. Running away to hide would be difficult. They decided to stay where they were with Anu's sister, Aunt Klara and her family in Zdana. They would go along with the edict and pray the war would end before the resettlement was implemented. Apu's sister Kati and her husband Uncle Moritz also lived in Zdana. Uncle Moritz was a large man with a ruddy face, a dark black mustache, and big strong shoulders. Although Uncle Moritz looked tough, he was actually gentle and good-natured. He decided it was time to leave Zdana. He knew a few peasant families and hoped they would help him. My brother Bondi said he wasn't leaving Aunt Klara or Grandpa Shimon. I didn't want to leave my brother and Grandpa, but I couldn't convince myself to stay and do nothing, just waiting to be taken. Bondi stayed with my grandparents and I joined Apu's side of the family.

It was quite a group that was leaving with Uncle Moritz. There were Gabi and I, Gabi's aunt and mother, Uncle Moritz's daughter Ella and his father Joe, Gabi's younger brother Andras, his grandmother Rella, my Aunt Kati, and two girl cousins of Gabi. We waited until it was dark. There was no moon that night; the only light came from the stars. Fortunately, Uncle Moritz grew up in Zdana and knew his way around. He took us into the woods along a narrow path. The forest was spooky,

44

so we kept close together. The path went uphill and down. It curved around thick tree trunks and you had to be careful not to fall over tree roots that made their way to the surface. Gabi and I stayed towards the back of the caravan. We walked for hours. While walking I prayed. I prayed that Uncle Moritz knew what he was doing and that all I had to do is stay with Uncle Moritz and I'd be safe. He was a woodsman and could name every tree in the forest with his eyes closed. But after we walked and walked till we couldn't walk any further, it felt as if we had walked to another country. Somehow we had only gotten to the next village.

Uncle Moritz took us to a farmhouse. He knocked on the door and convinced the farmer to let us in. I started to worry because I realized that our escape plan was evolving and hadn't been worked out beforehand. The farmer led us into a sitting room used only for company. There were rattan chairs and wooden end tables covered with doilies. The night was spent in that room, resting with our few belongings by our feet. In the morning the farmer announced that we had to go. Uncle Moritz begged him to let us stay at least until dark and gave him money for the favor. We couldn't risk being seen. The farmer agreed, but said that once it got dark we had to leave; he didn't want any trouble. There we were, sitting silently on rattan chairs in this sitting room. There was no talk about any future plans or how we were going to survive. As I bit my nails, all I thought about was how we were going to survive. The farmer's wife brought us warm milk in a pitcher right from the cow. We drank the milk with *babka* (coffeecake), the only food we took along with us.

Night came and the farmer chased us out. This time we walked along the side of the road. We looked like gypsies in the darkness. I stayed next to Gabi towards the back of the group. Suddenly, two policemen appeared from nowhere. It was like they were waiting for us. Maybe the farmer informed on us. Instinctively, Gabi and I jumped into a ditch off the side of the road. We didn't move or make a sound. I could hear people talking, but I couldn't make out every word or who was speaking.

"You're coming with us."

"We're just going…"

"Money? It won't do any…"

"I think there were more of them."

"I'm not sure. Let's look…here. Do you see?"

I could hear the policemen walking around in the dark and I held my breath.

"Maybe not. I think you're wrong. This is the whole bunch of them."

Within a few seconds the policemen gave up their search and the group quietly marched away. I was shivering.

"What do we do now?" I said to Gabi.

"We'll go to Slovakia. I have an uncle there who's a "big shot". He'll take care of us."

"How are we going to get to Slovakia?" I asked.

"Simple. We cut through the forest till we get to a railroad station. Then we get on a train and take it to Slovakia."

It seemed like a reasonable plan. What did I know? Gabi and I started walking towards the edge of the forest about 100 meters away. We stared into the dark forest and then looked at each other. As desperate as we were, there was no way we were going into that abyss. My eyes were asking, "Okay Gabi, now what do we do?" Gabi was sure of himself.

"Ervin, I know. We'll go back to Zdana. We'll go to the maid's house and from there we'll find out what's going on."

He was a year older than I and it was his town. I followed Gabi back to Zdana. When we got to Katka's house it was late and the lights were out so Gabi and I sneaked into the barn. We climbed up a ladder to the hayloft, which was like a large wooden crate perfect for sleeping. After being up for twenty-four hours I was exhausted.

I think it was Katka who came into the barn in the morning to milk the cows. She was in her late twenties and liked Gabi a lot. When we heard her coming, Gabi climbed down the ladder and told her what happened during the night. I followed behind him. Gabi asked her what she knew. She said that the Jews were in the school building, guarded by policemen. We asked her to go to the school and find out if our family was there. Maybe someone could tell us what to do. Katka knew everyone in Zdana including the police and was able to go in and out of the school without any problem. We were starving so Katka's sister Verona brought us breakfast.

When Katka came back she told us that our whole family had been brought to the school. They had a message for us: "Give yourselves up. Don't worry, you won't get in trouble for hiding. We're safe. All that's going to happen is that we'll end up in Kosice. We have family there and in Kosice we'll be fine until the end of the war."

It didn't sound like good advice to me. I remembered that the people deported from Humenne never came back from wherever they were sent, so I didn't want to join the family, but what choice did I have? Zdana was a small town and everyone knew Gabi. They knew he was a Jew and that I was his cousin. We couldn't stay with Katka very long. Gabi and I talked it over and eventually decided we would listen to our family's advice and give ourselves up.

In the school building Gabi and I split up. I joined my brother Bondi, Grandpa Shimon and Aunt Klara. Gabi sat with his mother, Uncle Moritz and the rest of his family. Bondi reminded me that Apu had a brand new pair of ankle boots sitting on a shelf in a closet at Aunt Klara's house. It was a shame leaving them behind in Zdana. Apu never even wore them. They were made from fine smooth leather and had a rich brown color with hints of red. I got a policeman's attention and told him about the boots. I told them they were mine and about how much I needed them. The policeman escorted me to Aunt Klara's house. I found the boots and stuffed some paper into the toe area for a better fit. They were beautiful boots. They stayed on my feet for weeks, until a *kapo* took them away from me in Auschwitz.

47

Chapter 14

Deportation - May 1944

Wagons took us to the train station in Czana. I traveled by passenger car back to Kosice where I was born. The local police and the *Nyilas* (Hungarian anti-Semitic Party) surrounded the city ghetto making sure no one could escape. Aunt Klara had a friend in Kosice and we moved into her apartment. Sleeping was tough because everyone had to sleep in one room and there were no beds, just blankets. There also wasn't much food around, so we got used to potatoes and noodles. Still life was bearable. I went to synagogue every morning and was surrounded by family.

The second day in the ghetto, someone knocked on our door. It was Erzi. She lived near Kosice and came looking for Bondi and me. I didn't know how she found us. (I found out later that Grandpa had sent her a note.) She hugged and kissed me and said she couldn't believe how much I'd grown. I told her about Apu getting sick and then his recovery, and the trip from Humenne, school in Mishkoltz, the walk through the forest, hiding in a ditch, my boots, everything. After listening to the whole story she asked what she could do to help. I wanted to ask her to stay with us or to get me out of the ghetto and take me to her home, but I knew it was impossible. Besides, we were safe in the ghetto. We just asked her to make sure that my parents were okay in Budapest. We gave her two feather quilts wrapped in paper to bring to my parents. They were hard to hold, but Erzi assured us that she would get the quilts to my parents and let us know how they were doing. Erzi didn't stay long. She hugged me and cried and for a moment, I thought she would take me with her. Erzi left with the quilts. I found out much later that she got them to my parents in Budapest.

We weren't fine in the ghetto. Two or three days later the Kosice ghetto was no more. I marched with 10,000 Jews to a brick factory just outside of town. Railroad tracks came into the factory and ended in a loading area. A barbed wire fence surrounded the factory. It was a perfect place for holding Jews. Each family claimed a corner of a drying shed. The sheds had thatched roofs held up by columns. There were no walls. There were also no bathrooms for us to use; just holes dug in the ground.

Grandpa Shimon built a wall in our shed to protect us from the wind that picked up at night. There was a soup kitchen, but this time we brought food with us from Kosice to supplement our diet. There were rumors that we were going to Poland. Then I heard that the Allies had bombed the railroad tracks and that we would stay in the factory. You didn't know what to believe. On my second day in the brick factory, the police took me with about two dozen people to a Jewish business in Kosice. We were picking up typewriters needed for the precise lists the Hungarian police used to keep track of prisoners. It was a difficult job for me, not because the typewriters were heavy, but because it was *Shabbos* and I was riding in a trolley car. It felt strange and I kept looking over my shoulder. I was waiting to be hit by lightning.

A few days later, a freight train steamed into the brick factory. Speeches were made in Hungarian. We were told that we were being resettled and that everything would be fine with us. Guards started shouting. "Quick, quick," they yelled in my ears. "Everyone into the cars, everyone into the cars." Wooden ramps were placed in front of 40 maroon cattle-cars. Soldiers with sub-machine guns and black boots stood above us on top of each car. Families pressed towards the train, moving up the ramps and through the doors. Some cattle cars filled before ours, and I watched soldiers slide the giant doors shut, locking them with a loud thud. I wondered if they locked the doors when horses or cows were the passengers. I walked up the ramp with my small bundle in my hand. Even though the day was overcast, it took time for my eyes to adjust to the darkness trapped in the car. Ninety Jews were packed into our car. Some people sat on the wooden floor and some stood. There wasn't enough room for everyone to sit at the same time, so we took turns. The doors of my car shut and the air was stagnated. Even when the train started moving, it was suffocating. Standing on a suitcase, Grandpa managed to remove a metal slat from the car wall near the roof to give us fresh air. There were two buckets in the car, one for water and one for waste. As the waste bucket filled up, it was passed to our part of the car and we poured it out the hole Grandpa made. We didn't talk much. Everyone knew we were in trouble. Every time I closed my eyes I saw huge vats of boiling water and Jews being pushed into the vats. Nazis were turning us into soap.

We stopped a few times on our way because the steam engine needed water. When we stopped, the door was opened just enough to let someone jump out to refill the water bucket. Outside, there were guards standing with submachine guns. At one station, a soldier holding a cloth bag and a gun climbed into our car. He yelled, "I want you to pass me all your valuables. That means money, jewelry, gold, silver, diamonds, watches." People went through their pockets. Women removed earrings and wedding bands. Men removed watches and cigarette cases. It was all passed forward to the soldier. It made perfect sense to me. Who needs jewelry showing up in soap bars?

Looking through small cracks in the wall, we tried to figure out where we were going. It was a long trip. I didn't eat or drink much because I didn't want to use the bucket. The motion of the train, the sound of the rails and the foul smell in the car made me nauseated. More than a day went by and we were still traveling. Suddenly, the train stopped. A hush went through the car. We weren't at a station; we were in a forest. Someone said that we were going to be taken off the cars and shot. It seemed very possible. We waited.

Finally, the car doors opened, this time wide. A soldier screamed into the car, "I want your valuables." No one moved. "I said, I want your valuables," he repeated. A few people yelled back, "We have nothing left to give." The soldier got frustrated. "Do you hear me Jews? Give me your gold." He pointed his gun into the car. Grandpa pushed towards the opening and jumped out of the car. "Listen. We told you. We don't have any valuables. They were already taken. You can shoot me, but we have nothing left." The soldier looked stunned. "Oh, all-right you old Jew. Get back in the car and shut up." Grandpa climbed back into the car. He was sweating and out of breath. The door slammed shut. I hugged Grandpa and then got him some water from the bucket.

Chapter 15

Birkenau

I could tell it was night when the cattle car stopped. I wondered if we were going to be let out or if it was just another station. The doors opened wide. On the platform, guards were yelling, *"Heraus,* (get out) *Mach schnell,* (move quickly)." This was it. Anxious to get out of the cramped car, I jumped to the ground. My boots landed in sharp gray railroad gravel. Grandpa and Grandma sat down on the floor of the car and slid to the ground. Dogs were barking, searchlights circling, everyone was screaming. A sea of people pressed and pushed and swayed. A strange smell was in the air, like burning feathers. There were barbed wire fences with high voltage wiring to the north and to the south. SS guards with blank faces screamed, "Leave your belongings. Form lines. Get moving. *Schnell, Schnell".* We walked towards the front of the train. Rising up from the ground I saw two fiery chimneys. Orange flames lit up the sky. My cousin Zoli asked pointing to the chimneys, "What do you think they're making in that factory?" "Soap. It's a soap factory," I said. "I told you, they're going to make soap out of us. But Zoli, I will refuse to bubble."

Four thousand dazed and bewildered arrivals from our transport walked towards the end of the selection platform in Birkenau. All around me, mothers, children, babies crying, guards screaming, and dogs barking. I stayed close to my relatives. I didn't want to get lost or trampled. We got closer to the front of the line. My brother Bondi was on my left, my grandfather on my right. Next to him was Aunt Klara, Edit and Zoli. Standing in front of us was an SS officer. The skin on his face was taut. Silver buttons stood out on his crisp green uniform. His black boots, holster, and gun glistened. In his hand was a riding crop tapping gently against his thigh. He looked us over without expression - like a woodsman selecting lumber. He sent Bondi left. He motioned for me to join my brother. I took two steps and stopped to look at Grandpa Shimon.

"What do you do for a living?" the officer asked my grandfather.

"I'm a pensioner," he replied.

"Good." The officer turned his riding crop slightly to the right. Aunt Klara pulled Edit close. They went right, Zoli to the left. It happened very fast. By the time I looked back to see where Grandpa was going, he was gone.

Zoli, Bondi, and I walked together. *Kapos* dressed in striped pants began screaming at us, telling us to march. They looked healthy and strong. They directed us into a large tent. They told us to strip naked and carry our shoes in our hands. I put my underwear, shirt, socks, and pants down carefully on the ground so I could find them later. Standing naked in front of strangers, I was too scared to be embarrassed. I was thinking differently. One by one we were shaved. First our heads, then our underarms and finally our pubic hair. The barbers were experienced. They did their work in silence. Why were we being shaved? I reasoned that hair wasn't good for soap. I stared at Bondi and Zoli. They no longer looked human. I wondered what I looked like. *"Mach shnell. To the showers."* I heard one of the striped pants prisoners say that we were going to be gassed. I was sure we were going to die. We stood under the showerheads. The pipes knocked and I closed my eyes ready for the end. Water sprayed into my face. I was given a clean striped jacket and pants. My clothes from home were left back in the tent. I realized I would never get them back, but at least I still had my boots. We stood in formation, one next to the other and five deep for hours. I was exhausted, thirsty, and hungry. Zoli was so weak that we had to support him so he would not faint while the guard was counting us. Finally, we were marched into Birkenau proper and packed into a large barracks. We were allowed to leave the barracks once to go to the latrine. The latrine was just a series of open holes in a concrete slab without any running water.

I learned fast that the strong and healthy prisoners in charge were *kapos*. They were usually German or Polish political prisoners, criminals or homosexuals. They could *organize* and get food and proper clothing. They ran the camp. One of the *kapos* stood near me. I said, "Do you know where my grandfather might be?"

"He's not in the barracks?" the *kapo* asked.

"No, he walked the other way on the platform."

"Then he's up the chimneys."

I didn't believe him.

Bondi and I climbed up a triple-decker wooden shelf in the barracks. Nine of us squeezed onto one shelf. We slept head to toe on our sides, all turned in one direction. I was exhausted and fell asleep immediately.

Night passed in an instant. Again, screaming. *"Heraus, heraus*, get up, get up, you lazy Hungarian sh--! *Schnell, schnell."* We went to the latrines. Still cursing, the *kapo* in charge again placed us in a line five deep. We stood at attention for *Appell* (roll call). A few conditions followed me everywhere. One was hunger. Another was exhaustion. And the third was *Appell*. We were standing to be counted - first by one overseer, then another, and then by the *blockaeltester*, the big *kapo*. It took hours and we couldn't stand any longer. A few of us sat down. One of the overseers started shouting, "Get up you lazy Hungarians. You. You have it easy. This is nothing. When I came here, it was ice cold and we stood in mud up to our asses, freezing. You see these barracks. When I got here nothing existed. We had to build it. Everything you see we built. And you complain? You're nothing. You're sh--. Now get up, or I'll whip you." We got up and they counted and recounted. Any time anyone sat down I heard this speech. I heard it so many times I knew it by heart. Not everybody listened to the overseer, so a few prisoners got whipped. It was hot and I thought I would die of thirst. Finally, a group was chosen to bring water. Two barrels of bitter water the color of coffee were brought. We got metal bowls. We were told that if we lost the bowl we wouldn't get food. I never lost my bowl. We continued to stand in the heat for a few more hours. Then we were sent back into the barracks. We expected to get some food, but none came. What did they want from us? We weren't doing anything, just standing, being counted, and starving.

On the second morning during *Appell*, I noticed one of the big overseers staring at me. Did he know me? The overseer came over and took off his shoes. Holding them in front of my face he ordered me to take off my new boots. He cursed and threatened me, so I gave him the boots. He was delighted. They were beautiful boots. The shoes I got in return were more like slippers, not my size, made of the cheapest materials, worn out and falling apart. My former life was gone.

On my third day in Birkenau, I got a new name. We were told to arrange ourselves in alphabetical order. Tables were set up. One at a time we approached the tables and sat down with our arms out in front of us. A prisoner with a hypodermic needle sat on the other side of the table tattooing numbers. Since cousin Gabi was also a Roth we were in line together. Gabi was first. He became A10490. On a piece of paper next to this number the prisoner wrote down Roth, Gabriel. Then I sat down. A10491 was pricked into my skin. Finally, Bondi became A10492. We compared our numbers. Mine was the neatest. I was branded like a horse, and I was happy. It meant that I was important enough to get a number. Workers get numbers, not people who go up the chimneys.

Chapter 16

Auschwitz I

We were starving. On the fourth day we marched out of Birkenau. We marched five abreast in a long line into another camp called Auschwitz I. Above our heads on top of the metal gate a sign read, "*Arbeit Macht Frei*." I learned what it meant. They will work us to death, then we'll be free. We entered a brick building and marched up to the second floor. Weak from lack of food, we climbed into the triple-decker bunks along the back wall of the room. While sitting with my brother, Zoli and Gabi on the top bunk, a prisoner walked into the barracks. All I saw was the back of his head. I jumped down and tapped him on the shoulder.

"Excuse me. Are you Bumi Gittelman…from Humenne?"

The man smiled, "Yes. Yes I am."

"I'm Ervin Roth. I'm here with my brother Bondi and two cousins."

"You're Yoshka's children, right?"

"Yes, that's right. I remember when you were taken. Have you been here since then?" I asked.

"Yes, I came in 1942," he answered.

"What do you do here?" I asked.

"I'm an administrator in the hospital. That's where I live." He pointed towards the stairs. "Wait here. I'll be right back."

Bumi disappeared. A few minutes later he returned. Two loaves of fresh bread were placed into my hands. Holding one loaf under my arm, I ripped off a chunk from the other and stuffed it into my mouth. I was so hungry I barely chewed. I ran to the shelves and climbed up to Bondi, Zoli and Gabi. It was like eating after *Yom Kippur*. I looked down from the bunk to thank Bumi, but he was gone.

The next morning, we were counted first by a *kapo* and then by a guard in uniform. After *Appell,* we were given black coffee and told to stand five abreast. The guard marched one hundred of us to a gravel pit near a river about two miles from the camp. The overseer prisoner in charge had a *pink triangle* next to his number on his jacket, indicating that he was a homosexual. He told us to fill a metal cart with gravel and to push the cart up a hill where we would unload the gravel. It was hot and there was no water to drink. Sweat blackened by the gravel dust dripped from my face onto my prisoner's uniform. I licked the sweat with my tongue and although it was salty at least it was wet. I worked slowly to conserve my strength. The overseer watched us from a shady spot near a tool shed. Every time I passed near him, I felt his eyes were on me. On my third trip to the top of the hill he came over and said he needed me to go with him to the tool shed. I figured that he needed me to get some more supplies. Inside the wooden shed were shovels, wheelbarrows, and pickaxes piled in the rear. The air was much cooler in the shed and it had a slight smell of petroleum. When I stepped into the shed the overseer followed me inside and pushed me gently with his hand. He closed the shed door behind us. It was dark inside, but beams of light poked through the cracks and joints between the wooden slats. As my eyes got used to the darkness, I saw the overseer standing in front of me. He put his arms around me. He pulled me close and hugged me tightly. Cool lips kissed my sweaty face and neck. I was inside away from the hot sun. For a few minutes I didn't have to shovel gravel or push the heavy cart up the hill. Being in the shed with the overseer was a relief from work. A half-hour later he told me to take my shovel and return to the gravel pit. I spent the rest of the day shoveling and unloading gravel. On the march back to the camp I didn't tell Bondi about the shed. It didn't matter. We were counted and recounted. Finally, we were allowed to go to sleep.

Chapter 17

The Kommandant

We lined up again for *Appell* and marched back to the gravel pit for another day of shoveling. After we made a few trips up and down the hill, the overseer came over to me. He was in a rush. I thought I was going to the shed again.

"I'm not sure what you two did, but you're in serious trouble," he said, pointing at Bondi and me.

"Us? We didn't do anything," I said.

"You must have, because you see that guard over there? He came out here to bring you to the camp Kommandant."

My brother and I looked at each other in disbelief. What could we have done? The overseer motioned to the guard.

"Put down your shovels and go."

We moved slowly. We didn't want to go. Some prisoners said, if the Kommandant wants to see us, we weren't coming back.

The guard ordered us to march. It was difficult for me to understand what was happening. There were thousands of prisoners. Why were we singled out? How did the Kommandant even know that we existed?

I asked the guard, "Do you know why we're being taken?"

He said, "I don't know, but I'm sure you must have done something." He walked behind us with his rifle on his shoulder.

Bondi and I already knew what Auschwitz was about. So we figured that we were either going to be punished with a beating or gassed. By the time we got to the Kommandant's office, we were as pale as ghosts and shaking. The guard took us into a large building and then directly to the Kommandant's office. He opened the door and said, "Wait here. The

Kommandant will see you in a minute." He walked out and closed the door behind him. We stood with our backs to the door, facing a massive wooden desk. Behind the desk up on the wall was a picture of Adolf Hitler. There was almost nothing on the desk, no papers, no books, not even a pen. Bondi and I stared at each other. We were frightened and we couldn't speak. All of a sudden, the door opened and cousin Gabi walked in with a guard. The guard walked out of the room and shut the door.

I whispered to Gabi, "Do you know why we're here?"

"I don't have a clue. I was working in the field and I was told to report to the Kommandant."

The three of us stood there in front of the desk shaking. A door next to the picture of Hitler opened and in walked the Kommandant. He was a strong, well-built man with a stern face. He came in dressed in full uniform: a hat, jacket, belt and holster with a gun. He unbuckled his belt, took out his gun and placed it on the desk without saying a word. He sat down and addressed Gabi in German.

"Where do you work?" he asked.

"The stables," Gabi answered.

"Do you like what you're doing?"

"*Jawohl* (Yes Sir)! " Gabi said enthusiastically.

"Do you like to work with horses?"

"*Jawohl*!"

"Do you like the food?"

"*Jawohl*!"

"*Gut* (good)." All three of you will be assigned to the stables. Dismissed!" He yelled for the guard. The guard came in. "Take this one back to work and these two prisoners to Block 13." Bondi and I were marched to Block 13 and Gabi was taken back to work. In Block 13 we were assigned to a bunk that my brother and I shared until January 18th 1945, the day we left Auschwitz on the Death March to Buchenwald.

I had no idea why we were summoned to see the Kommandant. I thought, maybe Bumi Gittleman would know what it was about. I had to wait until Sunday afternoon to see him. I walked to the hospital and found his office. Before I even said a word, he apologized and explained what happened.

My cousin Aliska was in one of the first transports to Auschwitz back in 1942. The Nazis were just setting up the camp and needed help to get things running. Because Aliska was fluent in German and knew how to type, she became a secretary working for a Major Liebehenschel. This was in Birkenau, before Liebehenschel became a "big wheel." Somehow, Liebehenschel got promoted to Lt. Colonel and became the Camp Kommandant. Aliska was reassigned to work for someone else who had something to do with new prisoners. When our transport arrived, she spotted our names and contacted her old boss, the Kommandant. She told Bumi to let us know that we could ask the Kommandant for any job in the camp. It's hard to know how things would have turned out if Bumi had reached us in time. He felt really bad. I told him it didn't matter; that I liked horses. I lied. I hated horses. But what could I say? Bumi was a nice guy.

Chapter 18

Odze

The head of our block blew his whistle at 3AM. I was asleep next to Bondi on our shelf. Even with the rest we got the day before, it was hard getting up in the dark. Everyone else in the camp got up at 5AM, but we were lucky; we worked with the horses. He ran through the barracks screaming, "Up. Up. Up!" like there was a fire. Then there was Heintz, the *kapo* in charge of our work group. The guy screamed like a maniac. He could scare the "living daylights" out of you. On his uniform was a black triangle, meaning he was a German criminal. They say he murdered his mother and father and maybe his wife, too. Nothing was for sure, except that he was a murderer and a homosexual. Heintz was crazy, but I never saw him hit anyone. He was a screamer, not a hitter.

By 3:30 AM we marched five abreast to the camp entrance. I read the metal letters on top of the Auschwitz gate backwards to myself. Either way, the inscription mocked my fate and I hated it. The *kapo* in charge counted us while we waited for the SS guards to come. The guards were irritated that they had to get up so early. They cursed at us as if it was our fault. The guard at the watch-station counted us again to make sure he knew how many prisoners were leaving the inner camp. On the other side of the gate we were counted again by the SS guards to make sure they received the right number of prisoners. It took a long time to complete the paperwork, but finally we marched to the stables.

The head of my stable was a kapo in his mid twenties named Odze. He was a Jew from Medzilaborec, a town only a few kilometers from Humenne. Odze was tall and lean, but strong, about 5'10" with dirty blond hair and a ruddy face. Odze was an organizer, with connections inside the camp. He could get food, cigarettes or anything else he wanted. In the stable, he handed me two metal bits. "Get your horses," Odze thundered. "They're out there." Odze pointed towards the pasture. It wasn't easy figuring out which horses were mine. It's not like you call their names and they come running. Eventually, I got my animals. Then I had to pry open my horses' mouths and push the bits between the teeth. I got bitten and kicked by the horse, but I finally did it. Now I'm standing between my horses pulling them along on a gravel road to get them back to the stable. We were supposed to stay on the right side of the road. My horses could sense I didn't know what I was doing, so they went left. I tried as hard as I could to get them to stay in line with the other horses, but they kept on moving left.

From out of nowhere, whack. Something hit me hard on my shoulder and neck. It felt like a rock or a hammer hit me. I touched my shoulder with my hand and checked to see if I was bleeding. I turned around and there's Odze, holding a pair of bits in his hand. "Keep your horses in line," he growled. He was a prisoner and a Jew like me. Under my breath I cursed him. I was hit many more times and harder by other *kapos*, but I remembered Odze.

Back in the stable, I cleaned and fed my horses. It was a whole process that took time to learn. The horses were valuable and the SS made sure they weren't mistreated. Horse care was a ritual. We had to comb the horses' hide with a special brush. But you didn't just comb and finish. Dust and dandruff would come off the horses' hair and get caught in the teeth of the brush. You had to tap the brush and shake out the dandruff. Then you had to line up twenty rows of dandruff from each horse before you could stop. Some horses, like Gabi's, had a lot of dandruff. My horses had very little. Gabi would sneak me a row or two whenever he could. That first day in the stable it took forever to get my twenty rows.

When I finished, I got a small piece of bread and a cup of watered down coffee for breakfast. After eating we lined up again with our horses and brought them out to the fields. My problems weren't over. Before I could start plowing, I had to fasten harnesses around the horses. I threw the harness on top of the horse's back and it slid off. I threw it again and it went over the other side. I threw it again and again. I wasn't getting anywhere, but I kept on trying. I must have looked like a clown in the circus. I lived in the city. What did I know about horses? An SS guard was watching me struggle. He got so frustrated, that he grabbed the harness out of my hands, threw it on top of the horse, and with a tug tied the strap around the horse's underbelly. The guard did the same for my second horse. He slapped the horses' sides and told me to get going.

After the war, I'm walking alone on a street in Humenne. Someone taps me on the shoulder.

"I hear you're telling people terrible things about me. Tell me why you're saying these things." Odze's eyes looked threatening.

"What am I saying?"

"You're saying I was...you're saying I would...that I was cruel in Auschwitz."

"All I'm saying is what happened. That's all."

"What did I ever do to you?"

"You hit me the first day I worked in the stable."

I could tell Odze didn't remember. How could he? He did a lot of hitting in Auschwitz. His eyes blinked a few times as if he was trying to picture me in the camps.

"Oh c'mon. It was Auschwitz for God's sake." Odze face was redder than usual. "Cut it out!" He pointed his finger at me. "I'm warning you."

"What are you going to do? Beat me up? Odze, we're in Humenne, not Auschwitz."

Odze didn't say anything more. He wanted to, but he couldn't. He just walked away. I wondered where he could go. Later, I heard someone killed him in Australia. It might be that somebody else remembered him from the camps.

Chapter 19

Potatoes

It was fall and the earth was hard. The wagons filled up slowly. It was getting late, so even though I was working with the horses, I helped. My fingers, caked with dirt, yanked potatoes from the ground and dropped them into a wooden basket. I didn't fill the basket to the top because I was weak and needed to conserve my strength. The sun set early and large shadows buried the potatoes deeper into the ground. We continued to dig into the night. Tired and grimy we finally finished, walking back slowly behind the wagons. Normally, the filled wagons went to a storage-house, but it was too dark. Instead, we parked them at the stables.

It just happened. No one said a word. At once, a hundred of us gathered around the wagons. We pulled our shirts out of our pants and stuffed potatoes under our shirts. Then we quickly tucked our shirts back into our pants. I was thin like a stick but with the ring of potatoes I looked like I needed to go on a diet. I marched back toward the camp thinking about what I would buy with my precious potatoes. I wondered if I could get some meat, or maybe some thick soup. A few slices of bread were more likely, but when you're dreaming, you can afford to dream big. The guards seemed not to notice the potatoes or the excitement. When we got to the entrance to the camp, the SS guard in front counted the group and walked through the gate. When he came out, the watch-station guard screamed, "Inspection!" Getting caught smuggling potatoes would get you a severe beating or even death. As soon as I heard "Inspection," I pulled out my shirt and let the potatoes drop to the ground. So did everyone else. The guards ordered us to turn left and move five steps forward. Everybody was shaking. I said *Shema* with my brother. Behind us lay a pile of potatoes carpeting the road. The guards didn't say a word. They brought us into the camp and we went to our barracks. I waited for the punishment. Nothing happened. The next morning I figured that we would be beaten. Again, nothing! The guards acted as if nothing had happened.

A few weeks later, we were plowing a field. It was tough work and we were exhausted. At the end of the day we were on the way back to the stables. I walked between my horses and felt as if I was going to collapse. Someone decided this is crazy. We're exhausted and these huge horses are doing nothing. They should be carrying us. What an idea! So we all jumped on top of our horses. It was great. I was sitting up there like a king. The guards said nothing. I'm thinking we should have thought of this a long time ago. But all of a sudden I hear a whip crack and the wagon in front of the group and the wagon behind us are flying. Our horses begin to gallop and we're riding without saddles. I'm holding on to my horse's head trying not to be thrown off and my *tush* is smashing against the horses back with every stride. By the time we returned to the stables I was black and blue. I could barely walk. All I wanted to do was lie down, but the horses had to be walked into the stable and brushed. "Clean them well," the guard said with a smile.

Chapter 20

Wehrmacht

A new guard showed up at the stable. He was short and skinny, with dark hair and dark sullen eyes. A rifle hung from his shoulder like the other guards, but he was different. He didn't wear an SS uniform; he was *Wehrmacht* (German army). When he looked at me, he looked me in the eye.

"Excuse me. Are you busy?" he asked. "I need to get some straw for the horses. Can you help me?"

The soldier didn't yell an order. He asked me a question. "Okay," I hesitated. It wasn't a good idea to be singled out of the group.

"The wagon's over there. Follow me," he said.

I noticed as I walked behind him that he walked with a limp. He took off his rifle and casually placed it into the wagon in front of the driver's seat. His face grimaced as he climbed into the wagon and pulled his left leg over the railing. I climbed into the seat next to him.

"How old are you?" he asked.

"Fifteen."

"Fifteen?" He scratched his head. "I'm new here. I got wounded, so they sent me here."

We continued silently along the road. When we passed Birkenau, he asked, "What's over there?" pointing at the smokestacks.

"The chimneys? It's where they gas people and then burn them," I said indifferently.

"You're crazy. It must be some kind of factory."

"No, this is Auschwitz. They do that here. You'll find out."

I could tell the soldier didn't believe me. He looked at me as if I was a child who would believe anything and he knew better. He didn't know that there were no children in Auschwitz.

We came to a field with a giant mound of straw piled high. The soldier brought the wagon close and I began loading the straw into the wagon. The job went slowly and it didn't look like I would ever finish. I didn't notice that the soldier had placed his rifle on the ground, grabbed a pitchfork and started loading the straw from the other side of the wagon. Working together the wagon filled quickly. I jumped onto the wagon a few times to press the straw down so that we could fit more in. The soldier helped me get on top. When the wagon was stuffed with straw I took a wooden beam and placed it lengthwise over the straw. The guard threw me a rope and I fastened it to both ends of the beam with knots. I threw the rope back down and the guard looped the rope around the bottom of the wagon and pulled the rope tight.

"I think we're done," he said. The soldier picked up his rifle and handed it to me. He jumped up and slowly pulled his bad leg into the wagon. I handed back the rifle and he placed it between us on the seat.

"I'm here to rest," he said, as he shook the reins. "But so far I haven't gotten much rest. Maybe I'm too good a soldier."

"This place doesn't allow for rest," I said.

We passed a grassy field and saw two guards kicking a ball back and forth.

"Do you like soccer?" he asked.

"I used to play all the time," I replied.

"Me too. I played left wing. How about you?"

"I played right fullback."

"I'm not sure I'll be able to play again, with my leg." He stroked his leg with his hand.

"I'm sorry," I said quietly.

He was silent and I was afraid to disturb him.

Back at the stables, I unloaded the straw. As the soldier was leaving, he asked me my name.

The next morning some machinery needed to be picked up from the railroad station. The soldier called my name and told me to get into the wagon. I climbed in and sat down next to him. He wasn't very talkative. Once we were out of the camp he slowed the wagon down and reached into his pocket. From his pocket he took out a piece of candy and handed it to me. I jammed the candy into my mouth. Saliva dripped from my lips. Embarrassed, I wiped my mouth with the sleeve of my jacket.

"You were right," he said.

"About what?" I asked.

"About the chimneys." He shook his head. "I don't know what you did that got you thrown into this place, but to me you're not a bad kid."

I nodded. I wanted to tell him things like, I'm a Jew and that I didn't do anything wrong except for being born Jewish. That my parents are in Budapest and I'm sure, sick with worry about my brother and me; that I'm being starved and worked to death. Still he was a Nazi guard with a rifle. And even though this guard didn't scream or yell orders at me, I couldn't be sure how he would react. It was too risky and the words never came out.

We arrived at the railroad station and went to the freight office. It was my first visit back to civilization. The place was busy. People were everywhere; walking, shouting, working, buying, selling, doing what normal people do. I tried to make eye contact with anyone I could. I prayed that someone would have pity on me, a young kid, dressed in a prisoner's uniform, emaciated, with my shaved head and dark rings under my eyes. Maybe someone would realize that I was just an innocent kid being punished without having committed any crime. But even though I was standing right in front of them, no one could see me; I was invisible. The Poles were being oppressed by the Germans too. Maybe they would try to help me? I saw some children on their way to school. Shouldn't I be going to school? I wanted to yell 'help', but I saw that no one would come to my rescue. The soldier took care of business and the machinery was loaded onto the wagon. We went back to the camp and unloaded the wagon. The soldier thanked me for helping, and I thanked him for the candy. I waited for the soldier the next day, but he didn't come. After a few days, I figured he was reassigned to a different work detail, but I still hoped I would see him again. About a month later I did see him. He was marching a group of prisoners past our stable. He was looking straight ahead. I heard him yell, "You lazy Jewish dogs; march faster! You think I have all day?"

Chapter 21

The Colt

Outside, it was gray and quiet. Six months had passed since I arrived in Auschwitz. It was late fall and the cold made my joints stiff and teeth chatter. My feet, tired and weak, tripped forward against the hard ground. Instead of marching I wobbled along. Through the stable windows I saw the glow of incandescent bulbs hanging from the ceiling. Sunrise wasn't for another two hours. Stable #4 had the pregnant mares and newborn colts. I felt good in the stable. It had a sweet smell and was warm from the animals. Whenever I could, I'd watch the colts play with their mothers. They'd rub their faces against their mother's bellies, close their eyes and seem to smile. A Polish man named Stefan was in charge. He was tall and strong, with wide-set blue eyes and short brown hair combed straight back on his head. Stefan was quiet and efficient, rarely raised his voice and didn't hit. For some reason, Stefan never forgot he was a prisoner, too. We entered the building and stood on the curved stone path in the middle of the room. There was a strange noise coming from a stall towards the back. It sounded as if someone was in pain. Stefan rushed to the back stall and we rushed after him. One of the mares was in labor. We crowded around to watch. The mare was lying down on her side. Stefan approached the mare cautiously and spoke to her in Polish in a low comforting voice. He stood above her and rubbed her flank with the palm of his hand. Slowly he spread her legs and reached inside her womb. The mare whinnied and Stefan jumped back.

Speaking to the mare, he said reassuringly, "I called the vet last night and told him you'd pop today. You sure did. Just a little earlier than we expected."

My eyes were fixed on the mare, my mouth wide open. Stefan turned around.

"The vet's on his way and there's nothing to do till he gets here so you might as well go clean your horses." No one moved. We were paralyzed. "Now go!" Stefan yelled and we ran to our stalls.

I barely started to comb my horse when the vet arrived. Again, we huddled around the mare to watch. I had never seen the birth of a colt and didn't want to miss a thing. The excitement made me forget I was in Auschwitz.

The vet was a Polish civilian, but spoke German. He noticed the circle of faces staring at him. "Why are you all just standing around here when I need help?" he asked. "You, over there, get me a pail of hot water. And you - get me some towels."

The vet and Stefan kneeled down to examine the mare.

"She's having trouble," Stefan said.

"I know. The colt is stuck. I think she's losing blood too."

Beads of sweat dripped from the vet's forehead. Neither Stefan nor the vet was smiling.

"I'm going to have to pull her out. I can't let this go on too much longer. God help us if either of them don't make it."

The vet stood up and began to shout orders in German. He was excited and speaking very quickly. I didn't understand exactly what he wanted, only that I was to bring some straw and someone else was to rub the mare's side. The vet motioned that he wanted a few of us to come close to the mare and hold her down.

"You and you, grab her legs and hold them apart. Not too hard. Just don't let her kick me. And you over there, I need you to reach inside with me and pull the colt's legs forward."

Nobody moved.

"What's the matter with you? Are you all deaf? They should burn you all! Don't you know how to listen to orders?"

Nervous and frightened we held the mare down. It wasn't easy. She was angry and in pain and tried to bite and kick. The vet kept cursing and sweating. He looked frightened. Finally, he and Stefan pulled on the colt's hooves and I saw the tip of a snout push out. The vet wedged his hand behind the colt's head and yelled, "Here I go." The mare brayed and the vet pulled hard. Out came a baby colt. It was bent with its legs crossed and wet with blood. The colt was lucky. It took a step or two and flopped down. Stefan grabbed the colt and the vet, still screaming, worked on the mare. It took time but the vet got her to stand up. Stefan held the colt in his arms and placed him back on the ground near his mother. The colt took a few more steps and with help found his mother's teat. I thought how natural it was for a child when hungry to search for his mother.

I took care of the colt for a few days. It seemed to get bigger every hour. I walked him around in the corral and made sure he suckled. Once or twice I tasted the mare's milk. It was sweet and watery. The colt rubbed against his mother's belly, and got tangled under her legs. The mare knew it was her colt and didn't seem to mind. My brother Bondi was watching, too. He was crying.

Not long after, the doors of the stable flew open. The albino guard in charge of stable #5 walked in. He was tall and thin, strong and young even though he had white hair. With his red eyes he looked like he was drinking. I was busy combing my horse and tried not to make eye contact. In a booming voice he yelled, "You come with me. I need someone to exercise a horse." When I looked up I saw he was pointing at me.

I dropped my brush. I froze for a moment.

"Move it. I don't have all day," he said. His red eyes flickered. I ran to the door and continued to run to stable #5.

The guard handed me a bit and yelled, "Get the horse and bring him out."

I was able to get the bit into the horse's mouth quickly and pulled the horse out to an exercise square. I walked by the water trough and through the entrance gate. The guard walked behind me and shut the gate. He stood in the center of the square and was holding a whip.

"Walk the horse," he said.

Standing next to the horse I pulled the reins forward. The horse started to walk. I barely went around once, when the guard yelled "Faster. Walk him faster."

I was half walking half running.

"Now trot. I want you to trot," he yelled.

I started to run and I heard the sound of a whip snap behind me. I saw the guard was smiling.

"Faster, faster," I heard. The whip cracked by my legs and then near my face and my back and my legs again. The horse started to gallop and I tried to run faster, but I couldn't keep up. I tripped. The horse kept going, pulling me along in the dirt.

"Okay. Enough. You can stop. The horse needs to rest." The guard was laughing. I pulled myself up from the ground and felt around to see if any of my bones were broken.

"Hey, you're not done. The horse needs to cool down. Start walking." The whip snapped.

Out of breath, in pain, and filthy I walked around and around the square.

Finally, the albino guard yelled, "He's done. Bring him back to the stable."

As I walked the horse back inside, I kept smiling and thanking God for my luck.

Chapter 22

Selection

Moshe was my age; he slept on the shelf below mine. He wasn't part of our transport; he came from Poland, from the *Lodz* ghetto. Moshe didn't know what happened to his parents. He had dark eyes and a small build. But even though he was small, he did his job just like the rest of us. On Sundays, when we marched back into the camp past the orchestra, Moshe and Bondi would slow down and stare at the musicians. The orchestra sounded good, but I didn't think about it too much. I was thinking about where we were marching. Every Sunday after work we went to the showers.

The first thing we'd do is undress and hang our clothes on a hook on the wall. There weren't enough hooks for everybody so Bondi and I shared one. Then we'd walk naked along a short narrow hallway. A prisoner was standing against the wall on our right holding a bucket filled with gooey soap. Each of us cupped our hands and dipped them into the bucket. With the soap dripping from our hands, we continued into another room where showerheads hung down from the ceiling. We stood naked, waiting for water to come out. After all of us were packed in the room, warm water poured down like a rainstorm. A week's worth of dirt washed off our bodies and flowed through the spaces in between the wooden floor planks down to the concrete slab below and finally, out through a drain. The shower lasted two to three minutes. Wet, we returned to the changing room to put on our striped prisoner's uniform. Even though my uniform was filthy, at least my body was clean and it felt good.

One weekday evening in September, we were marching back into the main camp. We had spent the day draining a swamp, the same work we had done for weeks. But instead of going to our barracks as usual, our *kapo* marched us to the showers. We didn't even slow down. He just marched us right to the showers.

"What's going on?" I said to Bondi.

"I don't know. Maybe they think we're dirty."

"I don't think so. I think it's no good."

"You think they're going to kill us?" Bondi asked.

"Could be. We've been standing here too long."

"Say Psalms."

"You say them. Have me in mind."

We got undressed in the wooden room with the hooks on the wall. But instead of walking right into the showers there was a backup in the hallway. We were filing into the room one at a time. My turn came. Standing on the right was a guard in a neat uniform with polished boots. Next to him was a prisoner holding a pad. I walked into the hallway and stood up as straight as I could. The guard waved me on to the showers.

I asked Bondi, "Did he take your number?"

"No," he answered.

"Good. He didn't take mine either."

"He took mine," Moshe volunteered.

He knew what it meant. We all knew what it meant.

"Oh," I said.

When we returned to get dressed there was an announcement: "If your name was taken you will receive bread tomorrow morning and you will not have to go to work."

On our way back to the barracks Moshe tapped me, "Did you hear what they said, I'm getting bread tomorrow?"

"I heard. Sounds good," I answered.

"And then I don't have to go to work. I can stay in the barracks," he continued.

"Yeah. It sounds real good."

We climbed onto the wooden shelves to go to sleep. Bondi and I were on the top shelf. Moshe's was on the bottom to the right. "I can sleep as late as I want, and you guys are going to have to go to work," Moshe said. He wanted to believe he was going to be okay. No one answered him. In the morning Bondi and I went to work and Moshe got to rest in the barracks. When we got back that night we found out that the prisoners who had their numbers taken were picked up around noon. Moshe was a nice kid and he was taken, so I was glad I didn't become such good friends with him. Even so it was hard not seeing him around. There really was nothing wrong with him.

A few months before, while I was working in the fields I started to feel dizzy. I told Bondi, and he said he also didn't feel so well. We slept on the same shelf, so one of us gave it to the other. We were lucky it was close to the end of the day. Otherwise, we probably wouldn't have made it back. We dragged ourselves into the building and managed to climb up onto our shelf. Our bodies shook with fever and we held each other close for warmth. All night my teeth chattered and my skin burned. My fever must have been very high because I thought I was under water. It was dark and everything was spinning. In my fever Erzi came to me. She brought me a washcloth for my forehead. But she never gave it to me; she just sat down on a chair in front of my bed and watched me rest. I called her, but she couldn't hear me because she was singing a song she used to sing to me when I was a child. She stayed for a long time.

In the morning I was exhausted. My muscles ached and my head hurt; there was no way we were going to be able to work. The *kapo* saw that we were still in our shelf, but didn't get angry. I didn't even have to explain. He looked us over and could see we were sick. He told us to go to the infirmary across from our building. I helped Bondi down from the shelf and we limped over. Outside the infirmary was a line of prisoners standing, waiting to be examined. We moved up slowly. Bondi and I had to lean on each other so we wouldn't fall. Finally we climbed the steps in front of the building. I was called into the examining room. A Jewish doctor looked down my throat and checked my hands and feet. It was the measles and I was contagious. The doctor told me to go to the hospital. Bondi had the measles, too. So together we made our way to the hospital. Inside, the *schreiber,* (office clerk) wrote our names down. The *schreiber* pointed us towards the patient ward. Even though I was sick, I knew it was smart to get a message to Bumi Gittleman. I was burning up with fever and shaky, but I walked back to the *schreiber*.

"Excuse me. Bumi Gittleman, do you know him?"

"I know him," he said.

"Could you tell him, please tell him that the Roth brothers are here in the hospital," I stammered.

"I can't just go deliver messages, but I'll tell him. Roth, I have your names."

"Please make sure."

"I said I would. Now go!"

I didn't think Bumi would get the message, but what could I do. We were assigned to a shelf in the ward. With difficulty, Bondi and I climbed up onto the shelf. We lay there the way we slept in the barracks, on our sides, holding each other. After a while, a prisoner came by with some soup for lunch. We swung our legs around on the shelf so that they dangled down and held out our bowls to get some soup. Our arms were twitching and the soup was no better than the watery stuff we got in the barracks, but it still felt good not having to be out plowing. Also, in the hospital you could get as much water as you wanted. I dozed off and saw Erzi again, this time arguing with my mother. I woke up when I heard someone calling my name. Standing in front of me was Bumi Gittleman with a loaf of bread in his hand. We were too sick to enjoy the smell or taste the bread, but just feeling it in my stomach was good enough. By the next morning Bondi and I were feeling a little better. There was nothing to do in the hospital so I spent the day listening in on other people's conversations. There were two prisoners below us that were talking so loud it was hard not to listen. Bondi and I named these two men the 'coughers.' They coughed so much it sounded like they had tuberculosis. Whatever they had, it was bad.

"Okay, okay already. I get the point. Big deal, back home you were a 'wheeler and dealer'. You own this and you own that. But what are you here? A "Nothing!"

"Listen to you. You don't have a toilet. Forget a toilet, you don't have running water. Here. Here in Auschwitz you're an organizer. On top of the world. I'll tell you what. You get me some extra food. And maybe an egg or a slice of meat once in a while, and you know that field next to my factory. Well, it'll be yours. When we go home, I'll draw up the deed. I mean it! What do you say?"

"I have to think."

"What's to think?"

"Who knows what will be if we ever get out of here. Besides, I'm sick. I need all the food I can get."

"You have more than you need."

"Says who?"

"Be reasonable. It's a good offer."

"I'll be the judge of that."

"There's no use talking to you. You're an idiot."

"I'm the one with the connections. I'm no idiot."

They started coughing so much they couldn't speak. But after a few minutes they continued where they had left off.

"Does that field have a house on it?"

"Sure it has a house. And it also has a stable for two horses."

"I'll tell you what. If you throw in a horse, you have a deal."

"Horses are expensive you know. But if that's what it takes, I'll throw in a horse."

"You've got a deal."

The coughers shook hands and smiled. Now they could go back to just coughing and spitting. They were more entertaining when they were fighting. Still, the best part about being in the hospital was seeing Bumi. He stopped by everyday around lunchtime and always brought us some extra food. But on our fourth day in the hospital, Bumi Gittleman showed up very early in the morning. He was in a rush and he didn't bring us anything to eat.

"Boys, get yourselves ready to go. You're discharged," he said.

"Couldn't we stay another day, just to make sure we're okay?" I was not happy to leave. The hospital was a vacation.

"Absolutely not. You must leave right now. Back to the barracks!"

"Okay, if we can't stay, we'll go." I wasn't going to argue with Bumi.

I went over to the *schreiber* to tell him we were discharged. He said, "I know. You're discharged." Bondi and I walked back to the barracks. That night I found out, right after we left there was a selection in the hospital ward.

Chapter 23

Resistance

I was alone with my horse way off to one side of the field. A summer breeze from the forest made the air fresh and cool. I loosened my horse's harness, stroked her head and looked into her eyes. "It's a great day. But not for work. You don't want to work, do you? I didn't think so. You want to play soccer; that's what you want to do." I kicked my foot through the tall grass.

"Up to the wing, cross it, to the goal." With a big kick I went down on my behind. As I got to my feet and dusted off my pants, I heard a noise that sounded like a truck engine. I looked around. The noise got louder and higher pitched. It was coming from the sky. Sirens went off and smoke began pouring out of special smoke generators set up around the fields. Guards gathered the other prisoners together. I was far away from the group so no one came for me. I stood next to my horse with my mouth open watching the planes above my head.

"Look. They're carrying bombs. They know we're down here?" I grabbed the horse's reins and whispered into her ear.

"Do you see them? They're going to blow the place up." The noise was deafening. The planes were right over my head. I put my fingers in my ears and waited for the bombs to drop, but nothing happened.

"They must be turning around. They've got to be lower down to drop bombs. They're going to come back."

But the planes vanished and the rumbling noise slowly disappeared. I stared into the sky praying they'd come back.

"What's the matter with them?" Tears welled up. "They come here; they see us and then they leave?" I couldn't understand why they didn't bomb Auschwitz. They were right above the camp. I was so sure they would and was depressed that they didn't do a thing. It was hard to get back to work.

A couple of days later the air-raid sirens went off again. I was hitching a horse to a wagon near the stables. The *kapo* yelled to get the horses inside. The planes were back. I worked fast to unhitch the mare, but the horse moved and wedged its harness buckle tight against the front plate of the wagon. There was a shovel in the wagon, so I grabbed it and whacked the buckle as hard as I could. The buckle popped into place and I pulled the chain through the eyelet. Just after I got my mare into the stable I heard a huge explosion followed by what sounded like a hailstorm. Debris pounded the roof like a large drum. It made the horses crazy, jumping and kicking, their hooves in the air smashing against the stable walls. The drumming eventually stopped and after 10 minutes we heard an all-clear siren. After quieting the horses, we went outside to see what happened. Rocks and debris were everywhere. There was a crater 50 feet across and 10 feet deep right in front of the Nazi guard's quarters.

I turned to Bondi, "You see, they can be killed, too."

"It doesn't make me happy to see people killed," he said.

"People? They aren't people. They're…" I looked around and then said quietly, "bastards"!

"It's good that the bastards are dead, but as human beings, it's not good."

"Wait a minute. You're happy or you're not happy? You can't be both."

"I'm neither. It all cancels out" said Bondi. " A Jew isn't happy even when his enemy suffers."

"I guess I'm not a Jew," I responded. "But if I'm not a Jew, what am I doing here with a number on my arm? You know what I think. I think you're crazy."

Bondi replied "At least I'm the same person who came into this place six months ago."

I walked away from Bondi; he made me angry. I was entitled to be happy. It didn't last long. I found out that the bombing was an accident.

The plane didn't mean to hit Auschwitz. The area was soon cleaned up and things went back to normal.

In October, while plowing I heard an explosion. This time I could see where the explosion occurred. It came from the chimneys, from the crematoria. I steadied my horse, but it was difficult because the explosion was followed by gunfire. Guards on motorcycles, on bicycles and on foot, were running all over the place. They were holding rifles and pistols, and they were shooting. A prisoner ran into my field and behind him was a guard on a motorcycle. My horse was jumping up and down. The guard fired 5 or 6 bullets and the prisoner fell to the ground. The guard rode close to the prisoner and from a few inches away shot him in the head. Back towards the camp I saw a dust cloud rising from the direction of the crematoria. Guards gathered us together and marched us back to the stables. Soon we found out that prisoners had blown up one of the four crematoria and then tried to escape. It didn't work out that well. Just about everyone was caught and even the few that made it out were spotted in the city and brought back to the camp to be hanged. As bad as the escape had gone, I figured it was good for me. One of the four crematoria was gone. They would have to work harder to kill me.

Chapter 24

Death March

"Do you know what this means?" I showed Bondi a German newspaper I found while cleaning the guards' barracks. "It means they're close. All we have to do is hide until they get here."

"How much longer do you think?" Bondi asked.

"I think just days because I've been hearing rumors."

"What kind of rumors?"

"That the guards are planning to blow up the camp. The Russians must be close."

"They're going to blow us up?"

"Or they may just take off and leave us. Either way it'll be soon."

On the 18th of January, as usual, early in the morning we marched from our barracks to the main gate and waited for the guards to take us to the stables. Guards came, new guards I didn't recognize. When we got to a fork in the road outside the camp, instead of going right, which was the way to the stables, we went left over a bridge. The rumors were wrong. They didn't blow us up and they didn't just leave. In front of us and behind us, as far as my eyes could see there were people marching.

"Where are we going," Bondi asked.

"Towards Germany," I answered.

"They're going to kill us."

"I don't think so. If they wanted to do that they would have done it already."

"It doesn't matter. We're going to freeze to death."

Bondi was right. The air was bitter cold and there was a layer of snow on the ground. My pants and jacket were worn thin and flapped behind me in the wind. As I marched, snow stuck to the bottoms of my wooden shoes. When I could, I stuck out my hands that I hid in my sleeves for warmth and scraped the snow off. The straw I stuffed inside my wooden shoes got wet and froze my toes. I couldn't feel the ground below. I just heard the noise of the snow compacting under my feet. My toes went numb. Even today there are areas on my feet that can't feel cold. Snow fell, which was good because I collected the flakes in my hands and licked them off with my tongue. We got no food or water during the march so the flakes were like manna from heaven. Not far from the road were rows of houses. I could see them clearly; brick with colored shingles framing picture windows and Christmas wreaths nailed to wooden doors. Smoke poured out of the chimneys and I imagined I was inside next to the fireplace warming my hands and feet. I took off my pants and jacket and stepped into a hot shower letting the water hit my face with my eyes closed. I saw the Christmas tree decorated with candles and angels, and in the kitchen, warm bread and pie lay on the counter. They were so lucky, the people who lived there. I spotted them peering out of their windows, but they didn't come outside to bring us coats or boots or pieces of bread. My group limped forward flanked by guards holding submachine guns who rode in cars on both sides of the road. After a few hours new guards came and relieved the ones riding near us.

"It's going to be a long march," I said.

"I can't make it. I'm freezing to death," Bondi replied.

"Of course you can make it. Walk on the inside closer to me. You'll be warmer." Bondi moved to my left. His lips were blue and cracked, and the wind shook his tall thin frame. Black rings circled his eyes, and his nose was red and dripping. I noticed how bad he looked; he was losing it.

"Bondi, look over there," I screamed in his ear.

"What?" Bondi tried to focus.

"Look." I pointed off to the side of the road where the snow was higher. A body curled up with a red ring around it was lying in the snow.

"He stopped walking. Bondi, that's what happens if you stop walking. You want to end up like that?"

"I'm too tired to walk."

"I don't care; keep walking."

"What do you want me to do?" Bondi moaned.

"Recite Psalms. From the beginning. I'll say them with you."

Together we said the first stanza, *"Ashrei haish asher lo halach*...(Blessed is the man who does not walk with the wicked...)"

Around 8 o'clock in the evening, we walked by a school building. Guards ordered us to go inside. Bondi kept saying "Thank God, Thank God over and over". It took time, but eventually Bondi calmed down. We were given a small piece of bread, but no water. We sat at children's desks and Bondi slumped over and fell asleep. I checked to see if he was breathing and I fell asleep, too. It was still dark when we left the next morning, but I could tell Bondi was feeling a little better. The second day of the march was like the first, but worse. We were hungrier and weaker. Also, there were lots of bodies on the sides of the road. Bondi and I walked, our shoulders touching every step.

"Keep going, keep going, keep going," I grunted as I walked. "We have to stop somewhere." Bondi moved his lips and I think he was still saying Psalms; he had no strength to talk. I hallucinated that I was baking nut torte and smelling freshly baked *challah*. I prepared every dish I ever ate. Occasionally, submachine gun fire interrupted my thoughts. At night before Bondi and I fell asleep we realized that we couldn't last much longer.

On the third day of the march in the afternoon, we arrived at a train yard near the city of Gleiwitz. It was a busy place with lots of railroad lines converging, with cattle and coal cars, passenger cars and a few piles of railroad ties - the kind my father sold. In front of me was a long train made up of 40 cars. Most were open metal coal cars with about 10 passenger cars dispersed in between. Bondi and I were still alive. It was difficult to get into the open coal cars because they had no steps and I needed a push to get through the door. For an hour we waited, packed in the car, shivering together. Finally, a whistle blew and the train started to move. The hundred prisoners in my car swayed back and forth. We hadn't eaten for twenty-four hours, and the only water we got was from the snow that collected on our hands and sleeves. Some people passed out and fell to the floor. At least we weren't walking. Bondi and I experimented with different techniques to keep warm; locking arms, hugging, marching in place, deep breathing, but nothing worked. Guards kept watch from their passenger cars, and I heard submachine gun fire a few times during the trip. Any thoughts of jumping out of the car were forgotten. Finally, we entered a small station past the town of Weimar, and were ordered out of the cars. I was shaking and dizzy, but managed to march with the rest of the survivors. Bondi was worse than I was, so I placed my arm under his armpit. In front of us stood a barbed wire fence and brick and wooden buildings. Together we entered the large metal gate of another concentration camp.

Chapter 25

Buchenwald – January 25, 1945

I walked through the hall naked. Jellied soap was slapped into my hand and I continued into the showers. Hot water hit my face and warmed my body. It was incredible to be warm. I opened my mouth and let some water go in. Some got swallowed and some I sprayed out like a fountain. Even though we were weak, it made Bondi smile. After the showers, we were told to continue in pairs through the doors in front of us; I thought it was to get new clothing. Bondi and I entered a long dark corridor with bare bulbs hanging from the ceiling. There were electrical wires and open pipes every few feet and no exit.

"What is this place?" someone asked.

"The gas chamber," someone answered.

The room went quiet.

"Does it look like this?" Bondi asked.

"See these pipes…it's a gas chamber," I said.

"You sure?"

I nodded.

"At least we made it this far," Bondi said.

"Yeah. But this is it. The end of the road."

"If it's the end, why did they make us shower?"

"I don't know. Probably you can't have dirt on you when they…"

"How long do you think it will take?" Bondi asked.

"I don't know. Probably a minute or two."

"We better say *Shema*," Bondi said.

"But we're naked!"

"It's allowed. Just cover your eyes and don't look down." I covered my eyes with both hands. When we said the word '*echad*' (implying the unity of God), Bondi drew it out like Rabbi Akiva. We weren't the only ones saying *Shema*. There was no crying or panic, just an empty feeling in my stomach. I looked around and smelled for gas, but nothing happened. Doors opened and sunlight poured in at the end of the corridor. We shuffled towards the sunlight and entered a large room with big windows. Through the thick panes of glass I stared at the winter sky and setting sun. I was seeing everything for the first time: the red sun, the window frame, Bondi's naked body casting long shadows on the cracked floor. His face was so thin. We were alive. I thought about how close we came to freezing to death on the march and how we could have ended up in the gas chamber, and that it all depended on luck. I whispered to Bondi, "Thank God, Thank God." Bondi smiled. He loved it whenever I thanked God.

Behind a wooden counter, prisoners handed out uniforms. They were too large because we had lost so much weight. Still they were clean and disinfected. After we dressed, Bondi and I marched to a wooden barracks and were given new numbers. I was now number 119456 and Bondi was 119457. Chaim Sobel, the tailor's son would have been very proud of me. I stitched the new patch number on the left side of my jacket just the way he showed me.

We were counted and recounted. Four prisoners were ordered to go with a *kapo* while the rest of us stood in formation. They came back with two barrels of hot soup. We stood in line and waited our turn even though we were starving. The soup we got was not very good; it was mostly water. But I didn't care what it tasted like after so many days without food. It was a sign of things to come. Rations in Buchenwald were smaller than in Auschwitz. Bread was nonexistent. The facilities were nauseating, and disease spread quickly. There was also no way to *"organize"* (steal from the Nazis). After a few days, Bondi and I were sent to break rocks and carry them on our shoulders over to a pile. The hammers weighed more than we did. But breaking the rocks turned out to be easier than carrying them. If the guard didn't think you were carrying a big enough rock, he'd knock it off your shoulder and give you a *zetz* (whack). A prisoner next to me dropped the rock he was holding. The guard yelled, "What's the matter with you. Pick it up." The man bent down and tried to pick up the rock, but it was too heavy. "Didn't you hear me. Pick it up."

"I'm trying to," he said.

"You're not trying, you're a lazy dog." The guard beat the man with the butt of his rifle, hitting him again and again. Bondi and I watched, our eyes begging the guard to stop. The guard turned to us in anger and said, "You want to be next? Get back to work!"

At the end of February 1945 I was feeling depressed. I knew the war was going to end soon, but conditions in the camp were getting worse every day. Standing outside the barracks, I took off my jacket and turned it inside out. From the armpit I picked out lice. They were the translucent kind, with red dots in the middle and I snapped them between my fingers. In front of me, piled in a heap were the prisoners that died during the night. They were stacked like cordwood, the way Grandpa Shimon stacked lumber for railroad ties. Every night people were dying. A wagon pulled by prisoners came by and picked up the bodies. They were skeletons with huge dark eyes held together by leathery skin. I looked at my own body and realized that I was also wasting away. Still, as thin as I was, I wasn't a *muselmann* (walking skeleton). A *muselmann's* arms and legs were thin like sticks and you could see every rib. Their faces became brownish gray and their eyes would cloud over. Instead of talking, they whispered; they didn't move from their shelves. We called them *muselmanns*; I'm not sure why. That same evening, when I was going to sleep, there was a fight in the barracks. Someone yelled, "Let go of it. What do you need it for?"

Someone else yelled back, "Don't touch it. It's mine."

"Give it to me. What do you need it for?"

"Thief, let go!" I heard a struggle.

"Okay, keep your damned potato." Then it went quiet.

In the morning the older men in the block called a meeting. We found out what happened. A man in the barracks saw a potato bulging out of his neighbor's pocket. The guy with the potato was a *muselmann*. The man figured, what does he need with a potato? He's going to die anyway. But the *muselmann* caught him going into his pocket and grabbed his arm. They struggled and the *muselmann* didn't let go. Finally, the thief gave up.

But in the morning the *muselmann* was dead. The older members of the barrack decided that the *muselmann* might have died earlier than he should have because of the fight the night before. The thief had to be punished. They tied the man up and placed him on a bench. We walked by and spit at him. Most cursed him and a few hit him. We would not become what the Nazis wanted us to become – animals.

At the end of February we were standing in formation waiting to be counted. A uniformed guard came over to our group and began selecting prisoners. He was taking the older boys and men and separating them from the younger ones. Bondi was standing next to me. Even though he tried to stoop, he was still tall and had stubble growing on his face. The guard was getting closer.

"It's not good. Hide behind someone," I said.

"I can't. I stick out. Besides who knows what's best?"

The guard pointed at Bondi and said, "You!"

I grabbed Bondi's hands. "Don't go."

"I have to," he replied.

I looked Bondi in the eyes. My stomach was in a knot. How could this be happening? I knew this was bad. We hugged for a long moment and tears poured from my eyes. "Bondi, get back to the group. Sneak away. Listen to me." I was sobbing. Bondi didn't cry, but he looked scared.

"I'll be okay. Remember, everything is in God's hands," he said.

The guard was yelling, "*Schnell, Schnell.*"

Bondi walked towards the guard. He looked back and said to me, "Remember," and he pointed up to heaven.

I was worried about him staying alive and he was only worried about my soul.

Chapter 26

Last Days in Buchenwald – March 1945

Days went by. I waited for Bondi to show up, but he didn't. He might have tried, but just couldn't. Still, I kept expecting him to come back to the *Kleinlager* (small camp). I thought I saw him in the camp, tall and slightly bent over, gaunt with light brown hair. But it always turned out to be someone else. Without Bondi, the days were longer. I had to work without him next to me. My job was carrying rocks to one place and then carrying them back again. Bondi never cared if work was useless. All that mattered was fearing God and doing *mitzvos* (good deeds); everything else was useless. I didn't agree. Life was fine; it was carrying rocks I hated. The nights were harder than the days because that's when I had time to think. There were fifty kids on a large wooden shelf next to me, but without my brother I had no one to talk to. When I said the *Shema* at night, I knew God wasn't listening to me because Bondi was gone. We said the *Shema* together every night. Bondi told me that in the *Torah* it says that two witnesses are needed for proper testimony. Now, one witness was missing. For a while I stopped saying the prayer, but then I figured that Bondi was probably somewhere lying on a shelf like mine and saying the *Shema*. So every night, before I prayed, I asked God to find Bondi and put our testimony together. It didn't seem as if God was so busy in heaven anyway?

Conditions in the *Kleinlager* got worse - less food and more disease. The soup was mostly water and even that we didn't get every day. I was 5' 8" tall and weighed less than 75 pounds. My arms and legs were like broomsticks and my eyes were dark and recessed. Many people died during the night. In the morning, the piles of dead bodies in front of the barracks were getting higher each day. It was only a matter of time. The only thing working against the *Malach Hamaves* (Angel of Death) was the *blockaeltester*. Before the war he was a medical student. In the camps he was a political prisoner, a non-Jew, in his early twenties with black hair and a light complexion. I don't know why, but he wanted to keep us alive. Maybe it was because of his medical training; more likely it was because somehow some people manage to keep their humanity even in hell. One night the *blockaeltester* brought one of his friends into the barracks holding a violin. A real violin was smuggled into

Buchenwald. His friend was a musician and he played a piece of music he composed in the cattle-car that brought him to the concentration camp. I stared at his fingers sliding up and down the neck of the violin. They looked just like Bondi's fingers; thin, long and quivering. The music was wasted on me. What did I know about violins? Tears rolled down my face. How could I enjoy the music? I'm a soccer player. Bondi's the musician. I prayed that somehow Bondi would hear the music and find his way back to the *Kleinlager*. I wanted to believe it could happen. But when the music stopped, I didn't see Bondi - just a violin held by a stranger. I couldn't stop crying.

The *blockaeltester* became a father to us. He saved lives just by asking how we were doing. Knowing someone cared prevented you from giving up hope and becoming a *muselmann*. One day in March the *blockaeltester* came into the barracks excited and shouting, his hands waving above his head.

"Listen to me. Everyone listen to me." We quieted down. "I have a treat. My friend here is a mathematician. He's going to give a class now. I want everyone to listen. The subject is geometry." It was hard to concentrate. I didn't have enough strength to sit up so I listened lying down on my shelf. The mathematician was a good lecturer and he kept my attention. He was also in his twenties, thin and awkward, with a loud voice.

"What is a triangle?" he began. "Of course you know it's a three-sided figure. There's a relationship between the sides and the internal angles. Now what is this relationship? Any triangle with the same angles is a similar triangle, and we know a lot about similar triangles." He continued for an hour, proving geometry theorems as he went along. I don't remember the proofs, but I do remember for that hour I didn't think about food. I forgot I was starving. I forgot how weak I was. I forgot about everything. I soared out of the camp up above the electrified fences and floated through triangles, isosceles, equilateral, acute, and oblique. It was crazy teaching geometry to this group of half-dead prisoners, but it saved my life. It gave me hope. One day I'd get my life back. I would go back to school. I'd study geometry and when I'd go home for lunch, Erzi would be standing outside waiting for me.

A few more weeks passed and Bondi didn't show up. I gave up hope he'd come back. At the end of March "evacuations" started. This time I knew what it meant. I had been evacuated from Auschwitz, so I did whatever I could to stay where I was. The first few days weren't hard. When I heard the guards coming, I hid with a few other kids in a dark corner of the barracks away from the door. Because the *Kleinlager* was at the bottom of a hill the guards must have already filled their quotas from the other barracks so they didn't even bother coming inside. They just screamed from the road and I didn't move.

The next day the guards needed more prisoners so they came into the barracks. But they stayed in the center aisle so I was still safe crouching in the shadows. On the third day the searching began for real. I couldn't stay where I was. Outside, I noticed that there was a small space between the floor of our building and the ground; a perfect hiding place. I crawled underneath and waited. Bondi would have given me a tough time. He didn't like squeezing into tight places. He would have wanted to stay in the barracks and let God protect him. I heard the sound of the guard's heavy footsteps above my head as they got everyone out of the barracks. There were a few other kids hiding with me. The rats living under the building probably weren't happy we moved in, but it was a good place to hide. It was cool down there, and I could see what was going on outside. This spot worked for a few days. But it was risky being so close to the guards.

The next day I decided to hide in the latrine. The air inside was foul and the floor disgusting. It was perfect. The guards stayed away and besides, if they came for me, I'd jump into the waste. It worked until April 10.th. While hiding in the latrine, I heard noises coming from outside. First growling, then sniffing and scratching. The door to the latrine flew open. Black dogs with thick paws entered, barking and leaping, pulling fiercely at their leashes. I saw red wet tongues twisting and sharp white teeth snapping and spraying saliva into the air. I thought I would be ripped apart. Guards entered - leash in one hand, submachine gun in the other. There was nowhere to go. I threw up my hands and surrendered. They could easily have killed me for hiding, but instead I was just kicked and cursed. Maybe it was because I gave myself up without any trouble or maybe Bondi pulled some strings. They marched me to a large *Appellplatz* (parade ground) where I joined thousands of prisoners standing in formation. As I waited to be marched out of the camp, I knew I was in trouble but I tried to remain positive. I reasoned that even though I'm weak, the weather is better than it was when I was marched out of Auschwitz. Where are they taking us? It could be the same place as Bondi. Maybe if I find Bondi he'll have some bread for me. Still, I'm much weaker than before, and maybe I won't end up finding Bondi. How will I make it to another camp without my brother Bondi? I was making myself crazy, when all of a sudden the air raid sirens went off. Planes were coming over the horizon and in a flash the guards were gone, running to bomb shelters. We were left standing there. One guard not far from me didn't run. He pulled his revolver out of his holster. I covered my head with my arms and hands. I heard shots fired, but not at me. I looked up and I saw a guard shooting at the planes thousands of feet overhead. I started to laugh; this was the *uebermensch's* (superman's) defense, the mighty Third Reich. They actually believed that they were invincible. The guard looked in my direction and saw me laughing. He pointed his revolver, but he was out of bullets. He used them up on the plane. He sneered and cursed and walked away. The air raid continued for hours, but with the gate locked and the fence electrified there was no place to go. Still laughing, I returned to the *Kleinlager*.

Chapter 27

Liberation - April 11th 1945

There were no explosions. I went to sleep and woke up the next morning waiting to be marched out again to the *Appellplatz*. Outside I saw the guards up in the watchtowers standing with their submachine guns pointed towards the ground. Hours passed and still there was no order to march. We waited. Our *blockaeltester* came into the barracks at 9 o'clock in the morning and told everyone to get down from the shelves and lie on the floor. He said the American army was close and some bombs might hit the camp.

I imagined bombs blowing apart the fences, watchtowers falling, guards running in fear. It was too good to be true. I lay on the floor and listened for explosions. Many times before, I thought I would be saved and each time I was wrong. Not only didn't it get better; it always got worse.

But this time it felt different. At 10 o'clock someone noticed the guards in the watchtowers were gone. Where were they? Were they outside putting dynamite around the camp? I wasn't going to worry. Even though Bondi wasn't with me, I decided it was in God's hands. Getting hit by a bomb was also in God's hands, so I got up from the floor and went back to my shelf. I could wait more comfortably lying down on the shelf.

At 3 PM, two American soldiers walked into the *Kleinlager*. They were dressed for combat with boots, helmets, and rifles. One was white and the other black. The soldiers stood near the door and stared in at us. They didn't move. They just stood there staring. I was shaky, but I pushed myself up from my shelf. I wanted to get a good look at the soldiers, especially the black one. I had never seen a black man before. His eyes were yellowish, almost golden and his lips were dark red. His mouth was stuck wide open and he was breathing hard. His face was covered with droplets, not because he was sweating but because tears were running down his face dripping from his black cheek onto his leather helmet strap. I stood right in front of the soldier. He reached into his pocket and pulled out something small. He handed me a piece of chocolate. I put the chocolate in my mouth and the sugar rushed through my veins. It was hard to believe. They finally came. I reached out to touch the soldier's arm. Only when I felt the rough fabric of his uniform between my fingers did I believe he was real. The word *moshiach* (messiah) came out of my mouth. Two messiahs were in my barracks and one gave me chocolate.

Three hours later food came. Real food! Prisoners brought in metal barrels filled with thick pea soup and pieces of pork inside. I stuffed myself, filling and refilling my metal bowl. We ate as much as we wanted. My stomach was full for the first time in longer than I remembered.

Unfortunately, soon after eating I got bad diarrhea. My insides hadn't seen meat for such a long time that everything went through me. I had to keep going to the latrine. Even though my stomach hurt I was still euphoric. Pea soup with real meat - as much as I could eat, and just 50 feet away from the barracks, a water tank filled with clean water - as much as I wanted. The heavy food was a shock to my digestive system. Many boys got sick and were taken to a hospital set up at the camp. Some even died. That night there was plenty of room on the shelves.

A young Slovak boy with a dark complexion and straight black straw-like hair slept next to me.

"It's over," I said. "We're free. There's food and no more work and no more guards or rules."

"True, true." the boy answered somberly.

"You don't sound so happy," I said.

"No, I'm happy. I just don't know..." His voice trailed off.

"You just don't know what?" I asked sharply.

"I just don't know what will be next."

"We're going home to our families, that's what's next."

The boy didn't say anything more. He just looked at me with his sad brown eyes. I turned away from him to go to sleep and I thought of my home in Humenne, my mother and father, Bondi. It wouldn't be long now.

The next day we were given breakfast, and I tasted milk and white bread with jam and butter. My stomach was still bad, so for lunch I got rice and cereal and kasha. Before lunch I heard bad news that made my stomach hurt even more. The American President Roosevelt was dead. Things were going so well. Now who knows what will be? Will the next person finish up the war? Maybe he'll want to make peace with the Nazis and I'll be back in a concentration camp. I became depressed and didn't go out of the barracks. I couldn't get myself to walk outside. I was sad, alone, without my brother.

On the third day after liberation my feelings changed and I became desperate to find someone from home. I was still depressed, but now I had a mission. I walked between the different barracks and spotted a bunch of people surrounding an American soldier. He was speaking Yiddish and I listened and began to think.

"What kind of soldier speaks Yiddish? The soldier is a rabbi from New York. That makes sense. Wait a minute. My mother had a cousin who is a rabbi in New York. Could this be my relative? He looks the right age and build. Maybe it's Rabbi Wohlberg. Yes, this is what he would look like. Who would believe it? This man is Rabbi Wohlberg. God! You heard my prayers and sent a *malach* (angel) to take care of me. Bondi won't believe this. All I have to do is tell this *malach* my name and I'm set. He'll help me find my brother Bondi. Thank God. I like what you're saying Rabbi. The Jewish people will never vanish. This is a promise made to us by God Almighty. What's that? Your name is what? Rabbi Schachter? You're not Rabbi Wohlberg? You're not my mother's cousin? I have no luck and no relatives. Fine, I'll at least ask this Rabbi if he knows Rabbi Wohlberg. Wait a minute. Just because he's from New York, he should know Rabbi Wohlberg? I'm no small town kid that doesn't know how big New York City is! I'm not going to say anything. I'm not going to look like a fool."

I didn't and it was a mistake. Years later I found out that Rabbi Wohlberg and Rabbi Schachter were good friends and taught together at

Yeshiva University. I should have asked. He would have put me in touch with Rabbi Wohlberg right there in Buchenwald. I walked with the group surrounding Rabbi Schachter. We entered a building filled with people. In the crowd I saw someone from Humenne. It was Bunu Gross. He was with a friend of Bondi's, Meir Davidowitz. We hugged and cried. My depression made me think that I would be alone forever, that no one I knew had survived the camps. Here were two friends from before. There had to be others. The three of us decided that we would go back to Humenne to see who else survived. As soon as the war was over we would go home.

That night back in the barracks while lying on my shelf I started to feel strange. I was very cold and began to shake. By morning I was delirious. Somehow, I ended up in a hospital the Americans had set up, run by doctors who made it through the war. My fever was very high and I remember being wrapped in wet sheets. I thought it was typhus and that I was going to die. Imagine, I made it so far and then dying in Buchenwald *after* liberation. The world was turning in every direction so I just lay still.

Doctors visited. Sometimes what they said sounded slow and garbled. Sometimes it sounded fast and silly. In my delirium, Bondi visited. He asked me if I was still saying *Shema* and praying. "Who could pray at a time like this?" I said. "I'm busy you know. I'm sick." "I know you're sick," he said. "That's when you're supposed to pray." Bondi shook his head. Erzi sat at my feet wringing out washcloths. Bondi, stooped over and began saying Psalms. "Leave me alone. Leave me alone. It won't do any good," I cried. Bondi stopped praying. He was angry. "Stop it," he said. "You think you're so smart. You think you know everything. Listen to me. Say *Shema Yisrael* (Hear O Israel)! Now!" "Okay, *Shema Yisrael!*"

When I awoke I was drenched with sweat. Two days had passed. The hospital ward came into focus and the orderly changed my sheets. A doctor came by. I felt better. For dinner I was given thin soup. I was alive. But, an hour later, my fever was back up. I was nauseated and vomited. My stomach was killing me and my head was spinning. I was sure I was dying again.

This was what my life was like throughout the war. Things were bad. They would get a little better and look like they were going to be fine. Then poof, they would get even worse. This time, miraculously by morning the heaving was over. The Nazis were gone. I was free. I was alive.

Chapter 28

Adjustment

The first Sunday after liberation they came by train and they walked through the camp. Their heads were bowed and their lips silent. What could they say? They didn't lift their heads to look at us, but I looked at them. Dressed in their city clothes, clean, tidy, hair combed and shoes polished. I looked at these people with hatred. They lived only 7 kilometers from where I was standing. These people, the people of Weimar, saw us marching through the streets, defusing bombs, removing debris. Thin emaciated bodies walking past them. They were unmoved. When they saw the *Fuhrer,* they cheered *Heil Hitler.* When they saw their children dressed in the "Hitler Youth" uniforms, they cheered *Heil Hitler.* A concentration camp operated in their backyard, but they chose to look away. These bent, faceless figures were the remains of the proud German people, the *uebermenschen* of the Third Reich. The men were given shovels and ordered to bury the dead. The women in their Sunday dresses were forced to watch. The men dug and shoveled. Some of them barely picked up dirt, but the American soldiers didn't beat them. I wanted to go over to these people of Weimar and say; "Do you see me now? Am I still invisible?" I should have done it. There was so much anger inside me. I wanted to see justice carried out, but there was a problem. Who could find the murderers? There were so many of them. Who could identify them? The black soldier, the *Moshiach*, who cried in my barracks, he would find them. He would make sure justice was done. I could count on him. He saw our suffering. He saw what they did to us and he would never forget.

It was incredible how much I could eat. It seemed as if I would never make up for the food I missed. I wasn't getting sick from the food any more and I was getting stronger. It was hard to believe that I was really free. The nightmare had gone on for so long that even weeks after liberation, I wasn't convinced. Maybe this was all a dream or maybe I had died and this was just part of the process of traveling to the world to come. I would kick my shoe into the ground to see if it made a hole, or watch the clouds drift by over my head. I pinched myself to see if I felt pain. I would yell to another prisoner and see if he heard me. All just to make sure my liberation was real.

Days went by and I became restless and wondered what the rest of the camp looked like. I walked from my barracks to the perimeter fence. It was a strange feeling. After months of captivity, I could now touch the fence without being electrocuted. I could even walk out of the camp. Still, I never touched the fence and instinctively looked around to make sure there were no guards. Thank God it wasn't a dream; the guards were gone.

Beyond the fence was the crematorium. I decided to get a look at the place. I thought it would disgust me, but it was just a room with an oven, a piece of equipment. There were ashes on the floor and a few partially burned limbs in the oven. After months of seeing corpses piled high, the crematorium wasn't repulsive. It was just the way it was. If not for the Americans, that's where I would have ended up, a corpse in the crematorium - up the chimney. Still, it was strange to be in the room. Not because they burned bodies there, but because earlier, I would have been beaten for going somewhere I wasn't supposed to be. Now, I could go as I pleased.

There was an unusual room I heard about being set up in the camp and I decided to see it. I'm not sure who set it up. I think it was a political prisoner. The room had a few large glass test tubes standing on tables each filled with a clear liquid and pieces of skin with fancy ink pictures floating inside the tubes. I learned that Ilsa Koch, the wife of the former Kommandant of Buchenwald, had a hobby. She enjoyed making lampshades and other decorative objects out of tattooed human skin. Her husband would line up a few hundred naked prisoners and she would pick out the men with the most interesting tattoos. These men were killed and their skin processed like parchment. This too didn't seem that strange or revolting.

The Americans allowed us to live in the German army barracks. I moved in to my new home with three other Czech boys. It was as if I was vacationing in a gorgeous hotel. I had my own bed. There was a sink and closet. We even changed our prisoner clothes for German uniforms. A day or two later we decided we would take the narrow gage train into Weimar. My friends were intent on having a good time. We got out of the train and strolled along the main street. It was very busy. Everything looked strange to me. I watched a plump child eat an ice cream cone. His mother held his hand. Across the street a butcher shop had empty meat hooks in the window. Next to the shop, two men were arguing in German about the war. As we walked past, they didn't pause. They didn't look at us. I was still invisible.

"Excuse me," I said. "Do you know there is a concentration camp over there?" I pointed towards the camp. The men shrugged their shoulders and looked at me as if I was from Mars.

"Over there, there's a camp and do you know what they did over there? They worked us like slaves, beat us, starved us. They killed thousands. After that they burned…"

"We suffered too," one man cut me off. "You look better than we do." He went back to talking to his friend.

I wanted to smack these men. My voice cracked; I was breathing short breaths and I could feel blood rushing to my face.

"Hey relax, will you?" one of the Czech boys said. "What are you going to do, kill every German?"

I controlled myself. What was the use?

My friends weren't upset. They wanted to have a good time and I wanted to go with them, but I couldn't. I was suffocating. I had to return to the camp. I wasn't ready. What did I expect? That every German would say I'm sorry? That the people of Weimar would help me find my brother? I ran back to the train, back to Buchenwald.

Chapter 29

Reunion

Two weeks after Germany surrendered, there was an announcement that the American Army would provide transport vehicles to Plzen, Czechoslovakia. I thought about staying longer in Buchenwald, hoping that Bondi would come looking for me. But the Americans said it was more likely that if he were alive he would be on his way back home.

I left for Plzen with Bunyu Gross and Meir Davidovich, my friends from Humenne. The journey back home was different from the one to Buchenwald. The trucks had benches on both sides and plenty of "C" and "K" rations. Bunyu, Meir, and I could stretch our legs and eat. The trucks made a number of stops so we could rest and go to the bathroom. It was dark when we got to Plzen, so we spent the night in a boarding school dormitory. I slept in a bunk bed with a pillow under my head and a blanket to keep me warm. In the morning, hundreds of us boarded a train to Bratislava, Slovakia. Although it was the fastest way back to Zdana, it required a lot of walking. Most tunnels were bombed so we couldn't get through by train, but had to get out and walk around the rubble. At the other end of the tunnel we would pick up a new train. On one train, I sat across from a man who looked to be in his early 40's, wearing a brown leather jacket. He had black hair slicked back and a receding hairline. The train was packed with survivors, all boys around my age.

"Where are you from?" one of the boys asked the man.

The man didn't answer. He furrowed his brow and looked straight ahead.

"Were you in a concentration camp?" the boy paused. "I don't think so."

The man seemed annoyed and a bit nervous.

"You know what I think? I think you're a Nazi."

The man said nothing. He just kept looking straight ahead. But he was sweating now.

"How do I know you're not a Nazi? Do you have papers? You must have papers. You don't have papers do you? I definitely think you're a Nazi!"

The train pulled into a station. One of the boys ran out and called the local militia. When the man saw the militia coming he jumped out of his seat and ran off the train. We watched from the windows. The militiaman ordered him to stop, but he didn't. So the militiaman fired his gun. The man collapsed on the ground.

At another station I got off for some fresh air and when I returned to the train I was stopped. A militiaman grabbed my arm.

He said, "Where are you going?"

"Back on the train," I answered and pulled my arm away.

The militiaman was very suspicious. My blond hair had grown. I had gained back some weight and I was dressed in a German soldier's uniform.

"Let me see some identification."

I rolled up my sleeve and showed the man the number on my arm along with a certificate I got from the US Army. The militiaman apologized and let me back on the train. I wasn't nervous and actually found it funny that I was being mistaken for a Nazi. Now, having a number was a good thing.

It took a few days, but eventually I arrived in Kosice. It was as if I was retracing my steps back to my former life. I got off the train and walked into the station. My eyes searched the crowd desperate to find a familiar face. I spotted a middle-aged Jew who looked familiar.

"Excuse me. I'm trying to find my relatives. Their name is Roth. They're from Zdana."

"I believe there is a husband and wife by that name living in Zdana," the man responded.

"What does the man look like?"

"I'm not quite sure how to describe him. The man is tall, not heavy, with black hair. Maybe not black, but brown. I'm sorry, I'm just not sure."

"Is his name Yoshka?"

"Again, I'm sorry. I wouldn't know."

"My name is Ervin Roth. The man you described may be my father. Thank you."

My heart was racing as I got back into the train. My mind was racing too. Could it be true? My father and mother…alive? How will I find them? The train couldn't go fast enough. I stared out the window and saw only the faces of my parents. When the train pulled into the Mishle station, I ran the two kilometers to Zdana. At the edge of town I saw a man walking with a horse. I waved to him and he slowed.

"Do you know where the Roths live?" I blurted out.

The man took his time, looking me over from head to toe.

"The Roths?"

"Do you know where the Roth's live?" I repeated.

He pointed to a house.

It was Shoenberger's house. Aunt Pepi Shoenberger was my grandfather's sister. I ran to the door and stood at the entrance to catch my breath. Inside there was crying. Then I heard a voice say, "I expect a glass of wine when your children come home." Another voice said, "Not a glass, a liter." I opened the door and saw my mother sitting with a gentile neighbor crying.

"Hi Anu," I said as calmly as I could.

My mother let out a shriek and collapsed. The neighbor ran to get Anu something to drink and I ran to my mother. Anu revived and we hugged and cried.

"Ervinka, Ervinka, Ervinka…"

Anu's hands were shaking. She looked as if she was in pain as she asked, "Do you know anything about Bondi?"

It was difficult for me to speak.

Anu repeated more desperately, "Bondi. Do you know anything about Bondi?"

"We were together in Auschwitz," I said. "And then we marched to Buchenwald…together. After a while…in Buchenwald we got separated."

"Do you know what happened to him?"

"No. After we were separated, I didn't see him again. I think they marched him to another camp."

"Was he sick when you saw him last?"

"I guess he looked okay under the circumstances."

"What do you mean?"

"Anu, we were starving!"

"My babies. My poor babies." Anu began sobbing uncontrollably. I held her close and she cried on my shoulder. At some point the neighbor slipped out of the house.

A half hour later, my father burst through the door. "*Baruch hamechayeh maysim* (Blessed is God who resurrects the dead). Ervin. Ervin. Ervin." Apu ran into the room and threw his arms around me. My father never hugged me like that before.

"I knew it. I knew it was you," Apu said with tears dripping everywhere. "I walked into a store in Kosice," Apu continued. "And a man said to me, you are Roth, right?" I said "yes, I'm Roth."

"Then he told me. He told me that he thinks he just bumped into my son. He described you exactly. And I knew it was you. You were at the train station. So I ran to catch you, but the train took off just before I got there. So I hired a horse and wagon and Thank God…" Apu hugged me for a long time.

"Where is your brother, Bondi?" Apu eventually asked.

"I don't-"

"They got separated in Buchenwald concentration camp. Apukum, he's not sure where he is," Anu interrupted.

"I see," Apu said. "I see."

That night when I went to bed, I overheard my parents talking.

"Thank God he's back. I thought I would never see him again."

"But what about Bondi? Do you think he's alive?"

"I don't know? It's in God's hands."

"Yoshka, why didn't we send for the boys? They could have been with us in Budapest."

"We've been through this a hundred times, Ilonka. I was sick and we thought they were safer in the country, with the family."

"But we were wrong. No, Apukam, I don't blame you. You were sick. It's my fault. I am to blame."

"No. We didn't know. And Mrs. Farkash wouldn't have hidden them." Anu began to weep.

"Why are you crying? God willing, Bondi is alive. He'll be home any day."

"He's not coming home!"

"God forbid. Don't say that. You thought Ervin was gone and look he is sleeping next door."

"I won't sleep until both my babies are home."

My parents continued talking, but I was tired. I closed my eyes and said *Shema* and fell asleep.

Chapter 30

Anu's Stories

Slowly relatives came back. When they returned they never came back whole. My cousin Zoli met his father in Mathausen Concentration Camp and it was a good thing. Zoli was very sick. His father saved his life. His father carried him on his back until the end of the war. In Zdana, I was in charge of Zoli. First there was a boil to lance and dressings that needed to be changed. And then Zoli was diagnosed with typhus. He was quarantined and no one was allowed near him. The only thing Zoli would eat was sponge cake. I would bring him pieces of cake a few times a day and push it through a window. His mother, Aunt Klara, wasn't coming home. I knew that. I knew she didn't make it through the first selection at Auschwitz. I remembered Klara holding her daughter Edit tightly in her arms, refusing to let her go. Zoli's father was alone. He was unhappy in Zdana. Without his wife, he had nothing. And whom could he marry? There were few women his age that survived. He surprised us. He married a young girl Zoli's age whose parents never came back. Zoli couldn't understand it. Anu brought Zoli into our house. He was the son of Anu's favorite sister and inherited Klara's personality. We became as close as brothers. Gabi's mother also came back. But Gabi had vanished. In time we found out that he was in a hospital in Germany. He contracted tuberculosis and for months he stayed in a sanatorium.

Two months went by. The survivors stopped coming and sadly many relatives did not return. Anu's parents were gone. So were Aunt Klara and her daughter Edit; Aunt Malvene and her two sons, Herman and Zoltan; Apu's sister Ilush with her four children; Gabi's father Sandor and brother Andras; Kati's son and daughter, Tibi and Ella. Only four of the ten Shoenberger cousins returned. And worst of all my brother Bondi was still missing. Everyday I expected him to walk through the door just as I did, but he didn't come. With each passing day, my hope of seeing my brother diminished. Without Bondi I thought Anu would end up in a mental hospital. It didn't happen like that at all. Anu was different after the war. She was driven but not in a bad way. She was driven to help out.

I knew Apu would come up with ways to make money, buying and selling whatever he could get his hands on. Every bit of money that Apu made went for food. Whoever came back needed a home, so there were many hungry mouths to feed. Anu was responsible for all the relatives. She got up early in the morning and went to sleep late at night. She could not do enough. The house was cleaner than when Anu had a maid to help her and the food was delicious. In between all of her chores she was busy talking to everybody. Maybe from all the treatment and therapy she received before the war, she learned how to help others. It was the first time Anu was a mother to me.

Slowly, Anu told me how she survived with Apu during the war. She told me how sick Apu was and that when he was in a coma the doctors said there was no way he was going to recover. She told me about Mrs. Farkash.

"The doctors said I should pray Apu would pass away quickly. But Mrs. Farkash, the night nurse, said to keep talking to Apu, even though he was in a coma. Sometimes they wake up, she told me. And she was right. Apu did hear me. And he woke up and got better. I think I wrote you about it, right? But he got better just in time for the deportations. We went from one *tzarah* (catastrophe) to another. Then Mrs. Farkash came in one night and said to us, 'You know they're taking Jews away. You need a place to hide. I've thought about it. I want you to stay with me.' I told her there was no way. It was too dangerous. But this Seventh Day Adventist angel, wouldn't accept a no. So we made a plan. At night, I secretly unstitched our yellow stars and Apu and I just walked out of the hospital. We looked like regular Hungarians going out for an evening stroll. Mrs. Farkash was waiting for us at the door of her one bedroom apartment. Inside were her daughter and granddaughter. It was a crazy idea, all of us staying there with her. There was no place to sleep and little to eat, especially since we decided it was too dangerous for her to buy anything extra for us. The neighbors would have been suspicious. It's possible the neighbors knew something, because Nazis came to search the apartment a few times. Apu hid on top of the linen closet and I hid behind a wardrobe. It's a good thing neither one of us was fat. Mrs. Farkash had a son-in-law in the Hungarian Nazi Army. He came home once on a three day pass. Mrs. Farkash's daughter told him not to tell anyone we were there. Not only would it be dangerous, she said she wouldn't sleep with him ever again."

"Then bombs hit the apartment building. Apu and I stayed inside the apartment; we couldn't go to the bomb shelter. We were hiding. It was a miracle. The rest of the building was destroyed; the only floor left was Mrs. Farkash's. But there was an even bigger miracle. When the Russian army liberated Budapest, they searched the city looking for Hungarian Nazis to send to Siberia. We were liberated Jews. We had no reason to hide. The soldiers came to the apartment and found Apu. They told him to get dressed immediately and to prepare for a long trip. We knew what it meant. Apu survived typhus and the Nazis. Now he was going to end up in Siberia. Apu told the soldiers he couldn't go. He was very sick and contagious with typhus. The soldiers laughed at him. 'That's not a problem. We have a Russian doctor to examine you and we'll see how sick you are.' It didn't take more than five minutes. The doctor was there. In the middle of the examination, Apu turned to the doctor. 'My name is Yoshka Roth. I am a Jew. My wife and I have suffered from the Nazis. Our children are gone.' Apu begged the doctor not to send him away. I'm telling you it was a miracle. The Russian doctor stopped his examination. 'I am also a Jew. Do not fear. I am quarantining the apartment. No one will come for you. You will stay here with your wife.' Imagine, a Jewish doctor!"

Anu told me more stories. They were always about Budapest. She wanted me to know everything, so she repeated them. The details were very important. I knew what happened to my parents as well as what happened to me. A few times Anu asked me about Bondi, but she never asked me about what I went through in the camps. Even if she had, I couldn't have told her. I wasn't ready.

Chapter 31

Humenne

The village of Zdana had farms, cows, dirt roads and not much else. To find Bondi we needed to contact agencies like the Red Cross and the International Tracing Service. That meant letters, telegrams, and phone calls. We couldn't do it from Zdana. Zdana was nowhere. On the other hand, Humenne was a real city. It had a post office, telephones, and telegraph. Authorities could be contacted. Our chances of finding Bondi were better from Humenne. We also needed to make plans. My Uncle Harry in New York could sponsor us, get us visas and we could go to America. We had to get word to Uncle Harry that we were alive. Humenne also had industry. Apu knew the city and figured he could get a job. Lastly, Apu wanted to see his synagogue and find out which of his friends had survived. It was time to go back. My cousin Zoli would join us. His mother, Aunt Klara, and his sister Edit were dead. Zoli's father couldn't take being alone and became depressed. So it was better for Zoli to live with us. Anu and Apu adopted him. He was now their son. I didn't complain. Zoli was my age and I was missing a brother.

Back when we were deported, our neighbors in Zdana helped themselves to our possessions. Now that we were leaving Zdana, Anu went door to door to see what she could get back. Our closest neighbor had our linens and a carved wooden end table. Anu asked and they returned the items. But Anu noticed that the linens looked different. The monogram embroidered on the corners had been changed. The neighbor said that she just never expected us to return. The end table was untouched. It had a secret drawer with some money and stamps inside. When we got it back, Apu checked the drawer. The money and stamps were still there.

Before we left, I went to Kosice for the last time. I saw Erzi. She hugged me and cried and took out the leather wallet Anu gave her as a Christmas present years before. Inside, there was a picture of Bondi and me.

"I carried your picture around all the time," she said. "I'm going to keep it there. I knew you'd come home. I'm sure Bondi will too. Look at him, such a good-looking boy. I hear you're going to Humenne. It's not that far away. You will come to visit…with Bondi. I will miss you." Erzi cried. "Do you hear me? You'll always be with me."

"I know." I was crying, too.

Erzi hugged me hard and tight with her strong arms. I had thought about her a lot in the camps. She loved me like a mother and I thought she would somehow get me out of that hell. But she didn't come. No one came. I realized that she couldn't do miracles, that she had her own family and her own life, separate from mine. She was staying in Kosice and I was going home. When I was a child, she was my mother, but that was a long time ago. I never saw Erzi again.

When we got to Humenne, a Christian family was living in our house. The family didn't leave when we showed up. They stayed and we shared the house. They got the kitchen, foyer, pantry and a bedroom. We got three bedrooms. We didn't have a kitchen so we set up a little stove in one of the rooms. Anu and the wife worked together to keep the house clean and the husband helped chop wood for the stoves and heaters. Apu was out looking for work. The house wasn't in great shape after the war. Toilets were broken and a number of beams were cracked. There was a lot of work that needed to be done, but without Grandpa Shimon it wasn't going to happen fast.

I tried to help. Outside by the woodpile I picked up pieces of lumber. Each piece of wood I examined for smoothness, knots, and worms. I checked to see if the piece was straight or bowed. I breathed in the smell of the wood. It smelled like the forest, Grandpa Shimon's forest. Over my shoulder I felt Grandpa Shimon watching me. I needed his help to cut the wood, but now it was just me, the apprentice forced to learn by trial and error. He would have loved fixing up the house. Even more, he would have made me into a great craftsman.

Few old people over 45 or young children under 14 survived the camps. Mothers with babies didn't make it either. Most ended up in the gas chamber. But, there were a few kids between 15 and 20 years of age who returned. Many weren't from Humenne. They came from small villages outside of town because the villagers didn't want their Jews back. Many survivors who tried to go home were killed. So everybody went to the city. The teen-agers who survived found each other and went everywhere together. We became our own group and joined a Zionist youth organization called *Hashomer Hatzair*. We put on plays, talked about Zionism, played cards, and just hung out doing nothing. Officially, the organization wasn't religious. But in Humenne you could still be religious, go to synagogue and from there to a meeting.

Still, things were different after the war. Kosher food was hard to find and for months after liberation in Buchenwald, I ate "K" rations. I was still religious, but it wasn't like before the war. I didn't go to synagogue every morning. Coffee and toast at a café was okay. My group went swimming on *Shabbos* and no one said a word. Parents were afraid to say anything to their kids. They were just happy to see them alive. Even God looked different after the war.

I found out that Bumi Gittleman, the man who saved my life in Auschwitz, was living in Humenne. I was anxious to see him. Apu and I rushed to visit. Bumi was standing outside his house. I recognized him even from behind. He didn't notice us as we approached. When we got close, I turned to my father and said in a loud voice, "Apu, this man saved my life in Auschwitz."

Bumi turned around and was surprised to see us.

Apu said to Bumi, "Ervinka told me what you did and I want to thank you. It was a very heroic deed. Saving a single life is as if you've saved the world."

"Yoshka, please. I didn't do anything. Really, I did nothing," Bumi said.

"Apu, I told you, he brought me bread. I was starving and he...he watched over me like I was family. When I was-"

"You're making too much of this," Bumi interrupted. "The Master of the Universe watched over you. He watched over all of us. Thank God we made it through and that's it."

That's how Bumi was. He didn't want a reward or even a thank you. When we walked away I knew I had spoken with a righteous man.

"Heaven" may be filled with people like Bumi, but here on earth and especially in Auschwitz, I've only met a few.

Even though my parents wanted me to go to school, there was no way I was going back to the public high school. They didn't want me and I wanted no part of them.

Yolonka Friedman, one of the girls in my group decided she would go back. "It's different now; the Nazis are gone," she said. On her second day, when she got into the classroom, Yolonka couldn't find her desk. The window was open. She looked outside and there was her desk lying in the middle of the schoolyard. She ran out and never returned. My parents got together with a few other families and hired a couple of Jewish teachers. We studied hard and at the end of the year I took an exam and got school credit.

Occasionally I saw Sonia walking around. She was the girl I liked before the camps. Sonia was prettier than I remembered her. But I didn't speak to her. I couldn't. There was nothing for us to say to each other. Our lives took two different tracks and we were too far apart to ever meet again.

The Jews that returned to Humenne did not come back to reclaim roots and start life again. We were just waiting. Maybe another relative will come home from the camps. Maybe the quota to get to America will allow for one more family to get a visa. We were waiting to leave and the gentiles were anxious to see us go. Why should they have to move out of the house they bought at the auction? No, it was better for everyone if the Jews left. I lived in the city, but it felt as if I lived on the outside. The Humenne I knew was gone. It would never return.

My father's business was gone, too. Mr. Meleznik sold off all of our lumber and even our forests. He kept all the money and didn't give us a cent. He still had his own business and was now a wealthy man. The Nazis made it possible for him to take everything, and that's what he did. When he passed me in the street he tipped his hat. He wasn't embarrassed. He was like everyone else.

I got a present from Uncle Harry in America. It was a suit. Uncle Harry must have thought I was a giant because the suit was huge. I had to go to the tailor for alterations. It wasn't so simple. Sobel *bacsi*, the tailor never came back. He was killed, along with his son, Chaim and everyone else in his family. It was like they never existed. The same thing was true for our rabbi, Reb Ehrenreich, and our cantor, Reb Elefant, and the *shamos*, Reb Singer, and so many other people I knew and loved in Humenne.

Apu was out working hard to make a living. He supported us and he was sending money, packages of clothes and medications to Mrs. Farkash and her family in Budapest. This process continued through the years from America even after Mrs. Farkash died. Besides working, Apu was also busy writing letters and sending telegrams to the American Consulate in Prague. We were on the immigration list since 1938, but all the paperwork from before the war had to be redone. There were many setbacks. We had to redo everything. There was a quota. The U.S. only wanted physically and mentally healthy immigrants. We even had to appear at the US Consulate in Prague for medical examinations with a doctor to prove we weren't damaged goods.

Finally, in January 1947 more than a year and a half after the war ended, a thick manila envelope arrived. It contained four passports approved by the Czech government and four U.S. Letters of Immigration. You can't imagine the joy. Trying to get out of Europe for so long, made it seem like it would never happen. Now we had it in our hands. Apu immediately sent a telegram to Uncle Harry. The next day we received a telegram from Uncle Harry that he was arranging for our passage to America. Everyone should have an Uncle Harry. We soon received a package containing four tickets aboard the steamship Gripsholm sailing form Sweden February 1st 1947. In addition, Uncle Harry purchased tickets for our bus fare from Prague to Denmark, the ferry from Denmark to Sweden and the hotel accommodations in between. He even arranged to give us each $100 in Sweden before we boarded the Gripsholm. Uncle Harry didn't want us to arrive in America without any money.

In the midst of the excitement of leaving, Apu was still sending letters to the Red Cross, the International Tracing Service and the Allied Commissioner of Germany.

Dear Sir:
We are looking for our son Ondrej Roth. He was last seen in the Buchenwald Concentration Camp. He was taken from Buchenwald at the end of February 1945. We are looking for this person. Do you have information where he is or what happened to his transport? Please contact us at the above address. Thank you.
Yoshka Roth

The response we got from the different agencies was always the same:

We are still gathering files. As of now we have not found that name.

So much time had passed that it was unrealistic to think that Bondi would return. But we still hoped for a miracle. Maybe he was in a hospital with amnesia. Maybe he was wounded and in a sanatorium unable to get word to us. Jews live like this, always waiting and hoping. We were waiting for the day Bondi would return.

It was a cold day in January 1947. The sun was shining and we were happy there was no snow on the ground. Early in the afternoon we got ready. I wore the suit Uncle Harry sent me. Apu and Zoli were also in suits. Anu was wearing a dress and hat. Our suitcases were sent ahead to the train station. The four of us walked slowly to the station. I didn't cry or feel any attachment for my city. There was nothing left for me in Humenne. We were the first Jewish family to leave for America. News that we were actually leaving spread fast. Every Jew in Humenne came to the train station to see us off. They were a little jealous, but happy for us, too. We said good bye to our friends without tears. Many people screamed to us, "See you in America." It felt good - *America.*

The train pulled into the station and we climbed aboard holding on to our suitcases. We found seats and placed our luggage up on the racks. I took a window seat next to Zoli. The whistle blew and the train began to move. I looked back at my town, back at Humenne. It looked gray and old, decrepit, the kind of place you never want to visit. The poor Jews were standing around at the station, waving their hands, wishing they were the ones leaving on the train. I looked away. All I wanted to think about was America. I never wanted to see Humenne again. I elbowed Zoli and said, "Gut morning." It was the only English I knew. We both started to laugh. I looked over at Anu and Apu. They were both staring out the window. When they turned around, they had tears in their eyes. Anu said something to Apu. Apu held her close. Apu said something back and Anu started to cry. I wanted to hear what they were saying, but the train was rocking back and forth making too much noise. At first, I moved closer to listen. But then I realized I didn't have to.

Epilogue

The bus was hot inside, probably about 85 degrees even with air-conditioning. That's because it was 120 degrees outside. In 1963, that's as good as it got. During the hour ride I figured I had plenty of time to explain to my wife how electricity is made. I turned my head to the left and suddenly my lecture was over. My mouth dropped open. My heart raced and blood rushed to my head. My body went cold and I felt as if I couldn't breathe.

"What's wrong," my wife panicked. "Are you having a heart attack?"

I shook my head. I couldn't speak, so I pointed.

"What is it? Are you okay? What are you pointing at?"

"Him."

"Who?"

"Him. Him. Do you see him? Next to that blond woman."

"Of course I see him. Stop pointing. Who is he? Why are you so excited?"

"I think that's…my brother. I think it's Bondi."

"Your brother? You really think so?"

"Yes! I can tell from the eyes and forehead. Look, see how his eyebrows are different. One goes straight across and one goes up and then across."

"Are you sure? I thought he was dead."

"So did I. But you know, all we got from the Tracing Service was that he entered Bergen-Belsen. That's where it ends. Look at those eyebrows."

119

"I guess it's possible, but a lot of people have eyebrows like that."

"I don't know, it sure looks like him."

Because the air-conditioner was making a rumble I couldn't hear the guy's voice. I wanted to get up, but I couldn't get myself out of my seat. Just like this he's back. No warning, no letter, no phone call. It took me so long to get used to him being gone and now... Finally, I got myself up from my seat and moved closer to him. Now I could hear him pretty well. Damn it! Not a shred of an accent. His English was perfect. My stomach dropped. Still, I couldn't move away. This guy just looked too much like Bondi. He was good in languages. Maybe he got rid of his accent. Maybe his English is better than mine. "Bondi, look at me. Don't you recognize me? I look the same. I'm your brother." Nothing! This guy just kept talking and talking to the blond woman next to him. And what was he talking about? The weather! Stop with the weather already; your brother's standing next to you. You haven't seen him in eighteen years. Talk about Europe, your family. Talk about Auschwitz. Talk about being sick in the infirmary. Play the violin. Recite Psalms. Say *Shema*.

I stood in the aisle listening for a sign the entire trip. I studied the guy's face and mannerisms. Please God, make him say something familiar. In my head I rehearsed what to say, "Bondi, this is Ervin your brother. I've missed you." I stood for 45 minutes waiting. Still nothing. Not a single sign. He's too American. Too much a Yankee. The bus pulled into the parking lot. A sign said 'Welcome to Hoover Dam.' The doors opened and we slowly made our way out. My brother, the Yankee, disappeared into the crowd of tourists. It was terribly hot and I was sweating. My wife held my hand tight. I said nothing. As we walked, I heard the roar of the water passing through mammoth turbines and huge electromagnets. The noise was deafening. Against the giant concrete dam we looked like ants in search of food. I watched the calm river fall over the top of the dam in desperation into the placid lake below.

120

GLOSSARY

Appell – roll call

Appellplatz – parade grounds

Arbeit Macht Frei – Work Shall Make You Free (sign over entrance to Auschwitz)

Ashrei haish asher lo halach – Blessed is the man who does not walk with the wicked

Baal Koreh – accomplished Torah reader

Bacsi – uncle; often used instead of Mr.

Bais Hamidrash – house of study

Bar Mitzvah – boy's thirteenth birthday; he is counted as an adult congregant

Baruch hamechayeh hamesim – Blessed is G-d that resurrects the dead

Belzer Rebbe – the Rabbi of the city of Belz

Blockaelteste – inmate senior barracks supervisor

Chaim – life

Challah bread – Sabbath bread

Chasid, Chasidim (pl) – followers of a particular Rabbi

Cholent - stew

Chometz – leavened bread

Churban – defilement

Echad – implying the Unity of G-d

Gabbai – synagogue official

Hallel – Psalms of praise

Hamotzi – prayer before eating bread

Hashomer Hatzair – Zionist Youth Organization

Heraus - get out

Hlinka Guard – Slovak Fascist Party

Jawohl –yes sir!

Kapo – inmate concentration camp supervisor

Kiddush – blessing recited over wine before meals on Sabbath and festivals

Kleinlager – small camp in Buchenwald

Kohanim – heredity class of Jews to whom specific sacred functions are assigned

Kommandant – commander

Mach Schnell – move quickly

Malach – angel

Malach hamoves – Angel of death

Minyan – quorum of ten men required for group prayer

Mishnah – compilation of oldest post-Biblical Jewish law

Mitzvos – good deeds, meritorious acts

Moshiach – messiah

Muselmann – walking skeleton

Nuremberg Laws – anti-Jewish laws

Nyilos – Hungarian anti-Semitic Party

Orchim – Guests

Paskened – made a legal decision

Potch – smack

Rashi – famous commentator on the Bible and Talmud

Reb, Rebbe– short for Rabbi

Rosh Hashana – Jewish New Year

Sanhedrim – Supreme Court in ancient Jerusalem

Schreiber – office clerk

Sefer Torah – parchment scroll containing the first five books of the
              Bible

Shabbos – Sabbath

Shamayim – heaven

Shamos – sexton

Shema – prayer; affirmation of oneness of God

Shraim – left over food

Succos – Festival of Booths

Teffilin – philacteries: Two small boxes with leather strips, one wrapped
              around a man's arm, the other placed on the forehead during
              weekday morning services. Inside the boxes are selections from
              the Torah

Tish – table

Tosafos – additions – commentaries on the Talmud

Tractate Sanhedrim – Talmud dealing with the "Great Assembly"

Tzarah - catastrophe

Ubermench – master race; supermen

Wehrmacht – German regular army

Yom Kippur – Day of Atonement

Zetz – violent smack

ACKNOWLEDGMENTS

Heartfelt thank you to:

Rabbi Abner L. Bergman for his spiritual guidance and encouragement.

Susan Sussman, Abby Graphics LLC, who graciously designed the cover and photo pages.

Rabbi Martin S. Cohen, Dr. Mark F. Goldberg, Tina Tito, Terry Mangeri, Iris Schachter, Tom McGovern, Murray Dropkin, Ezra Dyckman, and so many others who read the manuscript and provided helpful comments and suggestions.

Donny Scharf for his technical assistance and advice.

George Horowitz for his calm demeanor, unstinting assistance in assembling the electronic documentation for *Bondi's Brother* and his generous spirit.

David Stollwerk for his friendship, understanding, insight and for meticulously editing the manuscript.

Cousins Gabi and Zoli for their stamina, fortitude, and resilience.

Addie Roth for her tremendous optimism, intelligent counsel and encouragement to complete the manuscript.

Robert, Candy and Lynne Roth for their patience, love and understanding.

Jessie, Jamie, Talia and Aaron Roth who make life exciting, enjoyable and great fun.

ABOUT THE AUTHORS

Irving Roth, Director of the Holocaust Resource Center – Temple Judea of Manhasset is a recognized speaker on anti-Semitism through the ages and the Holocaust. He is a frequent lecturer at colleges and universities in the United States and Canada. As a survivor of Auschwitz and Buchenwald, he also provides personal testimony on his experiences during WWII.

Mr. Roth received the 2004 *Spirit of Anne Frank Outstanding Citizen Award* from the Anne Frank Center USA for fostering human rights, social justice, and for conceiving, developing and initiating the *Adopt a Survivor* program. This program has been instituted nationally in public, and parochial high schools and colleges. He recently edited and coordinated the publication of a book titled *Adopt a Survivor – An Antidote to Holocaust Amnesia*. Mr. Roth has presented "papers" at Yad Vashem in Jerusalem, The Scholars Conference on the Holocaust and the Churches, CAJE (Conference on Alternatives in Jewish Education) and Facing History and Ourselves. He is the recipient of numerous awards for his work in Holocaust education and community service.

Mr. Roth received a BS and MS in Electrical Engineering from Polytechnic Institute of Brooklyn and resides in Nassau County, NY with his wife Addie.

Rabbi Dr. Edward Steven Roth received rabbinic ordination from Yeshiva University and is the founder and director of *Kesharim,* a Jewish institute of higher learning for college students. He teaches Jewish law and ethics at the institute and lectures on Jewish thought and philosophy in Queens and on Long Island. Rabbi Roth is the author of numerous articles and short stories. He recently completed an English translation of a Jewish medieval text on marriage titled *The Gate of Holiness.* He is presently writing a novel titled *Polemic on Long Island* and a mystical monograph on fundamentals of faith, *The Secret Foundation.*

Dr. Roth received a DDS from New York University School of Dentistry and completed a post-graduate program in periodontics at Columbia University School of Oral Surgery where he served as associate clinical professor of periodontics. He is a practicing periodontist in Kew Gardens Hills, NY where he resides with his wife Lynne and children Talia and Aaron.